Faulkner's Poetry
A Bibliographical Guide
to Texts and Criticism

Faulkner's Poetry
A Bibliographical Guide to Texts and Criticism

by
Judith L. Sensibar

with the assistance of
Nancy L. Stegall

 U·M·I Research Press

Ann Arbor / London

Copyright © 1988
Judith L. Sensibar
All rights reserved

Produced and distributed by
UMI Research Press
an imprint of
University Microfilms Inc.
Ann Arbor, Michigan 48106

17872739

Library of Congress Cataloging in Publication Data

Sensibar, Judith L. (Judith Levin), date.
  Faulkner's poetry : a bibliographical guide to texts and
criticism / by Judith L. Sensibar ; with the assistance of Nancy L.
Stegall.
    p. cm—(Studies in modern literature ; no. 94)
    Bibliography: p.
    Includes index.
    ISBN 0-8357-1879-4 (alk. paper)
    1. Faulkner, William, 1897-1962—Bibliography. 2. Faulkner,
William, 1897-1962—Poetic works—Bibliography. I. Stegall, Nancy
L. II. Title. III. Series.
Z8288.S46   1988
[PS3511.A86]
016.813'52—dc19   88-11077
                                                               CIP

British Library CIP data is available.

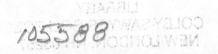

Ezra Sensibar
2 July 1905–16 August 1988
By love is he remembered and in memory he lives

Contents

Figures

Preface

This bibliography performs two functions. It gives the most complete descriptive listing to date of all William Faulkner's known extant poems, and it provides the first annotated bibliography of criticism of his poetry. The annotations cover all published textual, biographical, and critical studies through 1987.

William Faulkner began his career writing poetry. He practiced that art and craft devotedly for ten years (c. 1916–26). Yet only recently has serious attention been paid to this work which the young artist himself treated very seriously. In 1973, Keen Butterworth published the first "Census" of Faulkner's published and unpublished poetry (*MissQ* 26 [Summer 1973]: 333–59); it has served as the starting point for all inquiry into Faulkner's poetic apprenticeship. Building on the solid foundation of Butterworth's 25-page listing, the present bibliography records and reflects the immense growth in our knowledge of and interest in Faulkner's poetry over the past 15 years. Many poems have been recovered, identified, and published. Two major private collections have been given to university libraries. Perhaps the most significant discovery about the poetry as a whole is that it includes a substantial number of hitherto unidentified or unavailable sequences, sequence fragments, and poem groupings. With two exceptions (see below), these have all been added to or identified in university Faulkner collections and are listed in the bibliography in a separate section, "Published and Unpublished Sequences and Sequence Fragments."

Butterworth's 1973 observation that "study of Faulkner's poetry is important to understanding the prose style of his fiction" is now a given. In terms of the larger picture, Faulkner's verse illuminates the important relation of late nineteenth-century and early modernist poetry to the aesthetics of the later modernist fiction. These poems facilitate our understanding of the process by which, to paraphrase Pound, a generation of American writers made it "new"; thus, this bibliography serves as a resource both for Faulkner students and scholars and for anyone concerned with tracing the genealogy of modernist poetics.

In the listing of poems, I have inserted a section on sequences into Butterworth's basic organization, dividing the entries into published verse, unpublished verse, published and unpublished sequences and sequence fragments, and poem fragments. The fragmentary nature of many of the fire-damaged typescripts and manuscripts has made it necessary to depart sometimes from the usual methods of classification (by title or first line). When another method has been used, that information is included in the entry. A more detailed explanation of my entry format appears on pages xvii through xviii.

Major Additions to the Bibliography

The 1973 "Census" listed poems in Faulkner collections at the Beinecke Library, Yale University; the McKeldin Library, University of Maryland; the Berg Collection, New York Public Library; the Harry Ransom Humanities Research Center, University of Texas; and the Alderman Library, University of Virginia. Since then, the John Davis Williams Library, University of Mississippi, has acquired the Rowan Oak papers, originally housed at the University of Virginia, and the private collection of Douglas C. Wynn. Tulane University's Howard-Tilton Memorial Library's new poetry holdings are among the most important for they include the now published *Helen: A Courtship,* which Faulkner gave to Helen Baird Lyman in the 1920s, and several typescripts and manuscripts of poems and poem fragments that he may also have written for her.

Besides these new library collections, the private collector Louis Daniel Brodsky has published his copy of *Mississippi Poems* as well as illustrated catalogues and a bibliography listing of his Faulkner poetry collection. Brodsky's copy of Faulkner's [*Aunt Bama Poems*] has been transcribed, and copies of the original typescripts are available on aperture cards at the University of Virginia. Faulkner's daughter, Jill Faulkner Summers, has given the University of Virginia photocopies (the originals are, apparently, lost) of Faulkner's 1921 sequence, *Vision in Spring,* another handmade booklet (the [*Estelle Poems*]), and a poem Faulkner wrote in his copy of Ralph Hodgson's *Poems.*

These additions to the previously available poetry establish Faulkner's preoccupation with the poem sequence as his dominant formal structure. They have also increased our knowledge of Faulkner's methods of revision and made it possible to identify, date, and place previously undated or unidentified poems and poem fragments.

The most significant sequences (with the exception of *The Lilacs,* whose identifiable poems have all been printed as individual lyrics) have been published in trade editions. These are *Helen: A Courtship, Mississippi Poems,* and *Vision in Spring.*

Provenances of Various Collections

Many of Faulkner's poems originally came from a collection of charred manuscripts and typescripts recovered from a fire which destroyed Phil Stone's Oxford house in 1942. The majority of these were sold to the Harry Ransom Humanities Research Center at the University of Texas. Other known current owners of these Stone/Faulkner poems are the University of Mississippi and L. D. Brodsky. Much of the poetry in the Berg Collection at the New York Public Library came originally from William Spratling. He and Faulkner shared rooms in New Orleans in the spring of 1925 when Faulkner was writing *Soldiers' Pay;* the Berg poems probably date from that period. Most of the verse at the University of Virginia comes directly from Linton B. Massey, one of Faulkner's earliest collectors. Faulkner poems at Tulane, given by William B. Wisdom, belonged originally to Helen Baird Lyman.

With the exception of the Faulkner poetry in Brodsky's private collection, which is not available to scholars, I have seen all the materials listed. For the Brodsky entries I have relied on Brodsky's own publications. Where my descriptions differ from his, I have had the additional help of his published photoreproductions and some photocopies (courtesy of James B. Meriwether). I believe my revisions are correct as Brodsky, who asked for and was given the manuscript to review five months prior to press deadline, requested no changes.

I have also been told of another small collection of poems held by Carvel Collins in boxes at the Harry Ransom Humanities Research Center at the University of Texas. These are ["He furrows the brown earth, doubly sweet"], "Mississippi Hills: My Epitaph," and "An Old Man Says" (all in *Mississippi Poems*) and a group of poems that are bradded together and typed on legal-size paper in the following order: "April," "Vision in Spring," "Interlude," "After the Concert," ["Rain, rain . . . a field of silver grain"], "A Symphony," "Marriage," and "Philosophy." Versions of these same poems appear in *Vision in Spring* but in a different order. As I have seen neither originals nor photocopies of these typescripts, I have not listed them in the bibliography; I mention them here as they suggest the existence of another version of the longer sequence.

Discrepancies and Deletions from Butterworth and Other Prior Listings

The overall increase of 32 entries since the Butterworth "Census" does not accurately reflect the quality and quantity of Faulkner poetry now available. There have been almost 50 new publications of individual poems (a 75 percent increase in published poems since 1973), but the most significant publications in the past 15 years are the two sequences, *Vision in Spring* and *Helen: A Courtship,* and the grouping or sequence, *Mississippi Poems*. Also, many more versions of Faulkner's poems are now available. This has made it possible to identify many items listed previously under "Unidentified Fragments" and so shift them into other categories. In some cases I have been able to identify and reconstruct complete poems by matching fragments from different collections. Examples are "Mary Magdalen" (see figs. 29–30), "The London Mail," and various poems in *Vision in Spring*.

A few badly burned versions of poems in the "Census" have been deleted because, over time, they have simply disintegrated. Also, some poems have disappeared. Significant missing items are the original handmade volume of *Vision in Spring* and the [*Estelle Poems*], both of which are extant in photocopy (for the latter see figs. 33–34). Where necessary, the bibliographical descriptions of poems printed and discussed in *The Origins of Faulkner's Art* and Faulkner's *Vision in Spring* have also been revised and updated. Poems included in the Kinney and Fowler "Census" of the Rowan Oak papers have been similarly revised.

I have included illustrations to give readers examples of various problems and issues Faulkner's poems raise and to convey, as only his numerous reworked drafts can, the time and care he devoted to his poetry. Often, as with "The Ace" (figs. 1–3) which Faulkner wrote in his R.A.F. flight notebook, a titled, legible poem serves to identify untitled and otherwise almost illegible fragments; sometimes a page containing drafts of different poems (figs. 2–3), suggests which poems Faulkner worked on simultaneously. In some cases, matching up parts of poems from two different collections has given us a complete poem (see figs. 29–30). Leaves from two poem sequence fragments are illustrated in figures 35–40. But of greatest interest are poems like "Helen and the Centaur" (figs. 11–12), "Leaving Her" (figs. 15–18), or "The Gallows" (figs. 9–10) where, reading through the different drafts, one can actually see the young artist at work.

My thanks are due to Keen Butterworth and to others who have published checklists and written catalogues of various collections and library exhibits and to the staffs of the Beinecke Library, Yale University; the Howard-Tilton Memorial Library, Tulane University; the McKeldin Library, University of Maryland; the John Davis Williams Library, University of Mississippi; the Berg Collection at the New York Public Library; the Harry Ransom Humanities Research Center at the University of Texas; and the Alderman Library at the University of Virginia. Arizona State University facilitated this task by providing both a word processor and research assistants. I wish to thank David C. Hanson for his help in describing and cataloging the Wynn entries in the bibliography; Mark Olsen, who knows how to keep computers in line; and Nancy L. Stegall, whose assistance throughout is acknowledged on the title page. My colleagues, Willis J. Buckingham and O M Brack, Jr., read and commented on this manuscript in its earlier stages, and I am grateful for their suggestions. The errors are my own.

Editorial Method

Entry Format for the Bibliography

In this bibliography I have adapted the usual methods of classification to deal most clearly and concisely with the various problems Faulkner's poems present. The index lists poems with multiple titles under all titles as they appear in the publications, typescripts, and manuscripts; poems published with no title (as in *A Green Bough*) are indexed by first line.

The bibliography has four sections: "Published Verse," "Unpublished Verse," "Published and Unpublished Sequences and Sequence Fragments," and "Poem Fragments." Following the number of each entry is its title, if one has been assigned. If Faulkner has not provided a title, the poem is identified by first line, which appears in brackets.

If there is an original Butterworth "Census" notation ("A Census of Manuscripts and Typescripts of William Faulkner's Poetry," *MissQ* 26 [Summer 1973]: 333–59; rprt. in *A Faulkner Miscellany,* ed. James B. Meriwether [Jackson: University Press of Mississippi, 1974]), it is indicated in brackets so that readers may know which Faulkner poems were available in 1973 and which have been discovered and/or identified since. I use the following abbreviated notation system for Butterworth "Census" entries:

*PV: Listed in Butterworth as Published Verse.
*UV: Listed in Butterworth as Unpublished Verse.
*UF: Listed in Butterworth as an Unidentified Fragment.

After the title or first line of all published poems is a list of all versions, including reproductions and their sources and poems transcribed or quoted in full in critical works. The abbreviated references in these entries that are not italicized refer to the short-title listings itemized below; references that are not italicized and not fully notated refer to items listed in the annotated bibliography of critical writings at the end of this book.

I then list all extant typescripts and manuscripts of each poem. Entries include the following information: the type of document (how many pages and whether it is an ink or pencil holograph manuscript, a typescript, or a carbon typescript); the condition of the document (burned, fragment, number of lines visible and complete); the first visible line or phrase of all untitled typescripts and manuscripts; and any distinguishing features or significant information about the document. If a poem is part of a published or unpublished sequence, that information is noted, as is the document's present location.

All references to Brodsky manuscripts are cited by the entry number given in the 1982 Brodsky and Hamblin "Biobibliography" (see short-title listing *H/B 1982*). All references to materials at the Alderman Library, University of Virginia, and at the John Davis Williams Library, University of Mississippi, include an accession number to facilitate use of these large holdings. Manuscripts and typescripts at the Harry Ransom Humanities Research Center, University of Texas, are catalogued by first line and have no accession number.

Each of Faulkner's 14 extant published and unpublished poem groupings and/or sequences has been given a separate entry in the section "Published and Unpublished Sequences and Sequence Fragments." These are *A Green Bough, The Marble Faun, Helen: A Courtship, Mississippi Poems, Vision in Spring, The Lilacs,* the *Michael* Sequence Fragments, the [*Aunt Bama Poems*], the [*Estelle Poems*], the [*University of Mississippi Housman Sequence Fragments*], the [*University of Virginia Sequence Fragments, 1, 2,* and *3*], and the [*University of Texas Sequence Fragments*]. Titles of the first 7 groupings are Faulkner's. For easy identification and classification, I have arbitrarily titled and bracketed the last 7 groupings. In these entries, I describe all published, manuscript, and typescript versions of the collection or sequence as a whole, and I list their contents. Individual poems within each sequence have been listed separately, and I provide cross-references to the title or first-line entry under which each poem is listed. Due to the idiosyncratic nature of each sequence, the main entry includes a description of the sequence and of the approach I have taken in cataloguing it.

Short-Title Listings for Works Cited

The following short titles are used in this bibliography for periodicals, newspapers, anthologies, poetry collections, Faulkner novels, and critical or bibliographical works in which multiple publications of Faulkner's poetry or multiple reproductions of his manuscripts and typescripts have appeared. Also included are short titles used for book-length publications of Faulkner's poetry. All short-title listings are italicized to distinguish them from references in the annotated bibliography at the end of this work.

AGB	*A Green Bough.* See *TMF* and *AGB* listing below.
Blotner 1974	Blotner, Joseph. *Faulkner: A Biography.* 2 vols. New York: Random House, 1974.
Bonner	Bonner, Thomas, comp. *William Faulkner: The William B. Wisdom Collection in the Howard-Tilton Memorial Library, Tulane University: A Descriptive Bibliography.* New Orleans: Tulane University Press, 1980.
Braithwaite 1925	Braithwaite, William Stanley, ed. *Anthology of Magazine Verse for 1925 and Yearbook of American Poetry.* Boston: B. J. Brimmer Co., 1925.
Braithwaite 1959	Braithwaite, William Stanley and Margaret Haley Carpenter, eds. *Anthology of Magazine Verse for 1958 and Anthology of Poems from Seventeen Previously Published Braithwaite Anthologies.* New York: Schulte Publishing Company, 1959.
Con	*Contempo.*
DD	*Double Dealer.*
EPP	*Early Prose and Poetry.* Carvel Collins, ed. Boston: Little, Brown and Company, 1962. Contains all Faulkner poems published before *The Marble Faun.*
Gifts	Brodsky, Louis Daniel and Thomas Verich. *William Faulkner's Gifts of Friendship: Presentation and Inscribed Copies from the Faulkner Collection of Louis Daniel Brodsky.* University of Mississippi Printing Services, 1980. Catalogue from 1980 University of Mississippi Library exhibition.
H/B 1982	Brodsky, Louis Daniel and Robert W. Hamblin. *Faulkner: A Comprehensive Guide to the Brodsky Collection.* Vol. 1: *The Biobibliography.* Jackson: University Press of Mississippi, 1982. This volume includes all of the information which appeared in Hamblin and Brodsky's 1979 work, *Selections* (listed below).
HC 1981	*Helen: A Courtship.* New Orleans: Tulane University Press and Oxford, Mississippi: Yoknapatawpha Press, 1981. Unpaginated limited facsimile edition of 150 copies reproduced from photographs of the original hand-

	bound booklet in the William B. Wisdom Collection at Tulane University. Introduction by Carvel Collins.
HC/MP	*Helen: A Courtship and Mississippi Poems*. New Orleans: Tulane University Press and Oxford, Mississippi: Yoknapatawpha Press, 1981. Typeset edition of 1979 *Mississippi Poems* (Oxford, Mississippi: Yoknapatawpha Press) and 1981 *Helen: A Courtship* (New Orleans: Tulane University Press and Oxford, Mississippi: Yoknapatawpha Press) with reprinted introductions by Carvel Collins and Joseph Blotner.
James	James, Alice, ed. *Mississippi Verse*. Chapel Hill: University of North Carolina Press, 1934. Contains 7 titled poems that appear untitled in *A Green Bough*.
Lillabulero	The Spring 1967 edition (vol. 1, no. 2) of this Chapel Hill periodical reprints 5 Faulkner poems.
Man Collecting	Crane, Joan St. C. and Anne H. Freudenberg. *Man Collecting: Manuscripts and Printed Works of William Faulkner in the University of Virginia Library*. Charlottesville: University Press of Virginia, 1975.
Massey	Massey, Linton R. *"Man Working," 1919–1962: William Faulkner: A Catalogue of the William Faulkner Collections at the University of Virginia*. Charlottesville: Bibliographical Society of the University of Virginia and the University Press of Virginia, 1968.
Meriwether	Meriwether, James B. *The Literary Career of William Faulkner: A Bibliographical Study*. Princeton, New Jersey: Princeton University Library, 1961. Published record of the exhibition, "The Literary Career of William Faulkner," held in the Princeton University Library from May 10 to August 30, 1957.
Mis	*The Mississippian.*
MissQ	*Mississippi Quarterly.*
Mosquitoes	Faulkner, William. *Mosquitoes*. New York: Boni and Liveright, 1927.
MP 1979	*Mississippi Poems*. Oxford: Yoknapatawpha Press, 1979. Introduction by Joseph Blotner, afterword by

Louis Daniel Brodsky. Limited edition of 520 copies reproduced from typescripts in the Brodsky Collection.

NR   *New Republic.*

OM   *The Ole Miss, 1920–1921.*

OMY   *Ole Miss Yearbook, XXIV, 1919–1920.*

Origins   Sensibar, Judith L. *The Origins of Faulkner's Art.* Austin: University of Texas Press, 1984.

Perspective   Hamblin, Robert W. and Louis Daniel Brodsky. *William Faulkner: A Perspective from the Brodsky Collection.* Catalogue from 1979 Southeast Missouri State University exhibition.

Rowan Oak   Kinney, Arthur F. and Doreen Fowler. "Faulkner's Rowan Oak Papers: A Census." *Journal of Modern Literature* 10.2 (June 1983): 327–34.

Salmagundi   Romain, Paul, ed. *Salmagundi.* Milwaukee: The Casanova Press, 1932. This was a limited edition of 525 copies. It contains four poems previously published in the *Double Dealer* as well as the *New Republic* version of "L'Apres-Midi d'un Faune."

SB   *Studies in Bibliography.*

Selections   Brodsky, Louis Daniel and Robert W. Hamblin. *Selections from the Collection of Louis Daniel Brodsky: A Descriptive Catalogue.* Charlottesville: University Press of Virginia, 1979.

Soldiers' Pay Faulkner, William. *Soldiers' Pay.* New York: Boni and Liveright, 1926.

SoR   *Southern Review.*

SR   *Sewanee Review.*

Stylization   Hönnighausen, Lothar. *William Faulkner: The Art of Stylization in his Early Graphic and Literary Work.* Cambridge: Cambridge University Press, 1987.

TM   *The Marionettes: A Play in One Act.* Charlottesville: University Press of Virginia for the Bibliographical Society of the University of Virginia, 1978. Introduction and editorial apparatus (including complete bibliographic description of all extant manuscripts) by Noel Polk. This is a reissue of a 1975 limited edition (126 copies) which was reproduced from the University of Virginia manuscript. Its text is identical to another 1975 edition which was reproduced from the University of Mississippi manuscript (*Marionettes: A Play in One Act.* Oxford, Mississippi: Yoknapatawpha Press) and includes a prefatory essay, "A Memory of Marionettes," by Ben Wasson.

TMF and *AGB*   *The Marble Faun and A Green Bough.* New York: Random House, 1965. Reprints 1924 edition of *The Marble Faun* (Boston: The Four Seas Co.) and 1933 edition of *A Green Bough* (New York: Smith and Haas). Pagination in the original versions and the reprinted versions is identical.

VIS   *Vision in Spring.* Edited with an introduction by Judith L. Sensibar. Austin: University of Texas Press, 1984. An edition of Faulkner's 88-page poem sequence which he dated 1921 and hand-bound. Pagination of sequence is identical to author's typescript.

Wells   Wells, Oliver, ed. *An Anthology of the Younger Poets.* Philadelphia: The Centaur Press, 1932. Contains five previously published Faulkner poems.

Wilde   Wilde, Meta Carpenter and Orin Borsten. *A Loving Gentleman: The Love Story of William Faulkner and Meta Carpenter.* New York: Simon and Schuster, 1976.

Collections

The following system of initials has been used to indicate the location of documents.

Library Collections

CtY   The Beinecke Library, Yale University

LNT   The Howard-Tilton Memorial Library, Tulane University

MdU   The McKeldin Library, University of Maryland

MsU (Rowan Oak)   The Rowan Oak Papers, the John Davis Williams Library, University of Mississippi Library (also available on microfilm at ViU, accession #9817)

MsU (Wynn)   The Douglas and Leila Wynn Collection, University of Mississippi Library

NN-B   The Berg Collection, New York Public Library

TxU   The Harry Ransom Humanities Research Center, University of Texas

ViU   The Alderman Library, University of Virginia

Private Collections

JFS   Jill Faulkner Summers Private Collection

1

Published Verse

1. "The Ace"

Transcribed in *Blotner 1974:* 220.

    a. "The Ace," 1 p. penciled holograph fragment from 1918 R.A.F. notebook: 10 irregular, unrhymed and loosely rhymed lines; ViU (Accession #9817-b).

    b. Untitled, 1 p. penciled holograph manuscript: torn fragment, 6 lines; first line "He holds the world in his two"; on other side are drafts from "A Dead Dancer" (#24f) and a fragment of "L'Apres-Midi d'un Faune" (#7g); ViU (Accession #9817-b).

2. "Adolescence" [*PV:2 and *UV:20]

Third stanza quoted by Januarius Jones in *Soldiers' Pay:* 315; manuscript (a) reproduced in *Phoenix Book Shop Catalogue* 100 (Fall 1971): 10. The first 5 quatrains of this manuscript were also reproduced in *Faulkner on Fire Island* by Robert A. Wilson. This private publication of 250 copies, dated New York, Christmas 1979, was a holiday greeting from "Bob Wilson and the Phoenix Bookshop." On last page is printed "none for sale." Copies at NN-B.

    a. "Adolescence," 1 p. black ink holograph manuscript: 28 lines in quatrains; NN-B.

    b. "Adolescence," 1 p. black ribbon typescript on legal-size paper: 7 quatrains; "William Faulkner" typed and canceled bottom left; ViU (Accession #6074).

    c. "Adolescence," 2 pp. black ribbon typescript: burned fragment, 7 quatrains, all but 1 line complete; "William Faulkner" typed at bottom; TxU.

    d. Untitled, 1 p. black ribbon typescript: burned fragment, 22 lines visible, 15 complete; 2 ink holograph corrections; first visible line "Moon of death draw nigh"; TxU.

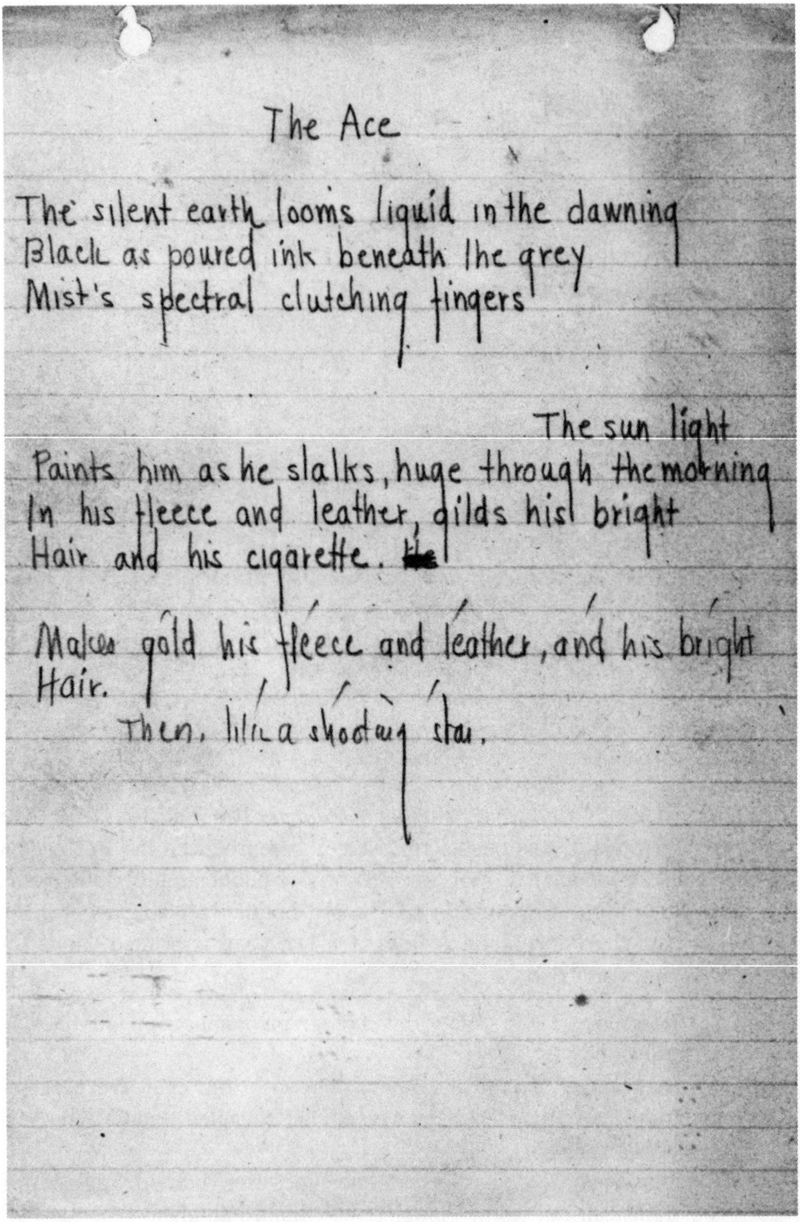

The Ace

The silent earth looms liquid in the dawning
Black as poured ink beneath the grey
Mist's spectral clutching fingers

                                    The sun light
Paints him as he stalks, huge through the morning
In his fleece and leather, gilds his bright
Hair and his cigarette.

Makes gold his fleece and leather, and his bright
Hair.
        Then, like a shooting star.

Figure 1. Holograph Manuscript Fragment of "The Ace" from
Faulkner's RAF Flight Notebook (#1a)
*(Courtesy Jill Faulkner Summers and the William Faulkner
Collection, University of Virginia Library)*

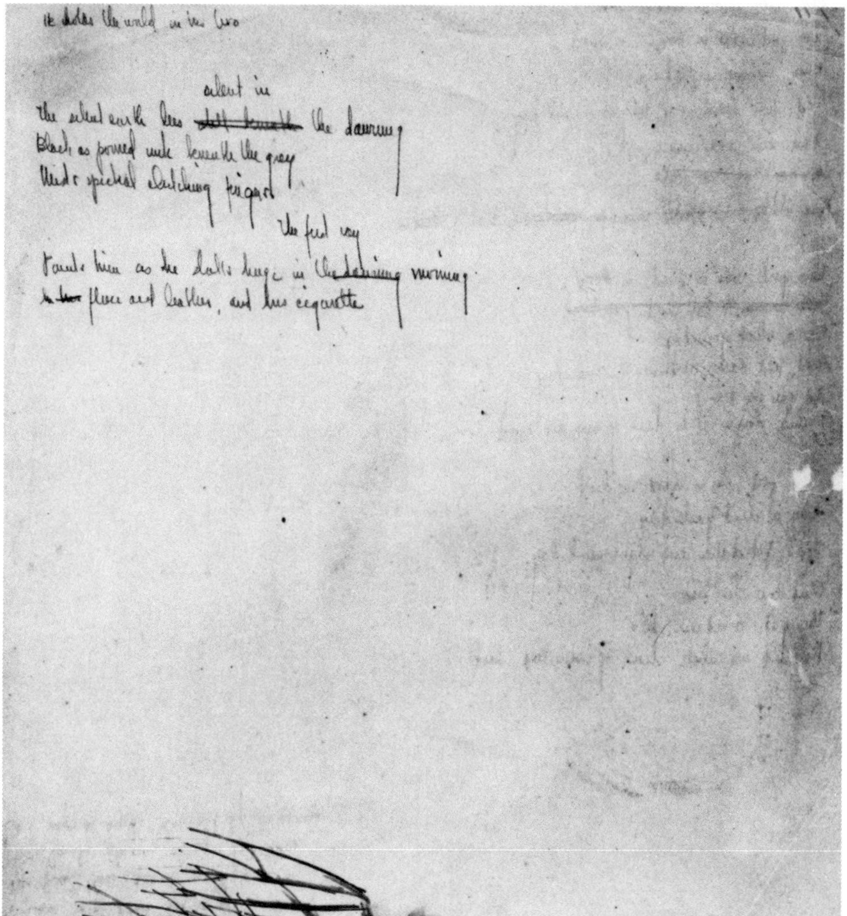

Figure 2. Holograph Manuscript Fragment of "The Ace" (#1b)
(Courtesy Jill Faulkner Summers and the William Faulkner
Collection, University of Virginia Library)

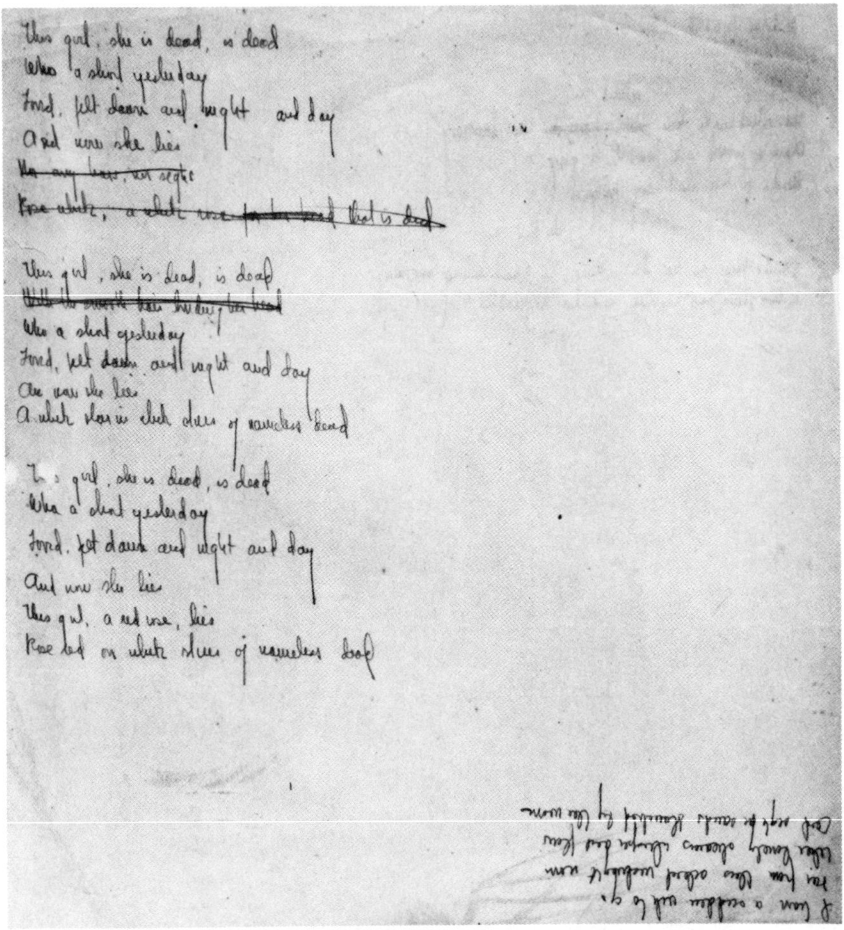

Figure 3.   Draft of "A Dead Dancer" (#24f) and Fragment of
"L'Apres-Midi d'un Faune" (#7g)
These fragments are on the reverse side of manuscript #16.
*(Courtesy Jill Faulkner Summers and the William Faulkner
Collection, University of Virginia Library)*

e. "Adolescence," 1 p. typescript: burned fragment, first 11 lines arranged in quatrains, visible and complete, but final line appears to be unfinished; MsU (Wynn, folder 5, #29).

f. Untitled, 1 p. typescript: burned but all 3 quatrains in this version complete; first visible line "Ah, spring, that with nightingale rose"; at bottom is typed "William Faulkner"; TxU.

3. "After the Concert" [*UV:3 and *UF:50]

   VIS: 30–32. Typescript (c) reproduced in *VIS:* Appendix B (p. xlii).

   a. "After the Concert," 3 pp. photocopy of carbon typescript: 39 lines; at bottoms of each page are consecutive numbers "30," "31," and "32"; this is *Vision in Spring* IV; ViU (Accession #9817-I).

   b. "After the Concert," 2 pp. black ribbon typescript: burned fragment, 32 lines visible, 26 complete; ink holograph "4." above title; TxU.

4. "After Fifty Years" [*PV:3]

   Mis 10 December 1919: 4; republished in *EPP:* 53.

   a. "After [Fifty Years?]," 1 p. manuscript: burned fragment, 15 lines visible; this is *The Lilacs* X; *H/B 1982:* 26, p. 27.

5. ["Ah no, ah no: my sleep is mine, mine own"]

   HC/MP: 121; manuscript also reproduced in *HC 1981:* n.p. The only known extant version of this sonnet is the *Helen: A Courtship* manuscript (#163), numbered "X" and dated "PAVIA-AUGUST-1925"; LNT.

6. "Alma Mater" [*PV:4]

   Mis 12 May 1920: 3; republished in *EPP:* 64. No known extant manuscripts or typescripts.

7. "L'Apres-Midi d'un Faune" [*PV:5]

   There are 2 complete extant versions of this poem. One version, Faulkner's first published poem, appeared in *NR* 20 (6 August 1919): 24. This was reprinted in *EPP:* 39–40 and in *Salmagundi:* 52–53. A second version was published in *Mis* 29 October 1919: 4. This also appears in *EPP:* 123–25. The first page of manuscript (e), and manuscript (f) in its entirety, are reproduced and discussed in Brodsky 1980. Typescript (a) transcribed in *Man Collecting:* 19.

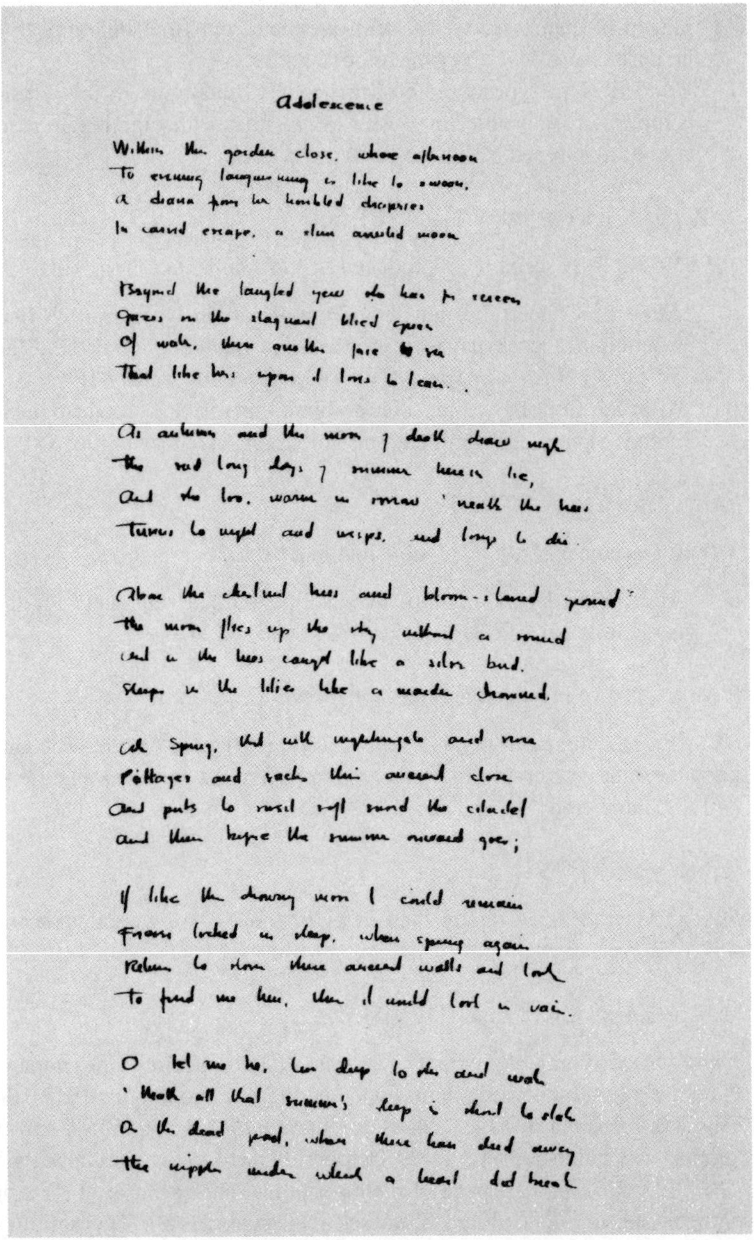

Figure 4. Holograph Manuscript of "Adolescence" (#2a)
Reproduced from *Phoenix Bookshop Catalog.*
(Courtesy Jill Faulkner Summers and Robert A. Wilson)

√ OK

Adolescence.

Within this garden close, where afternoon
To evening languishing, is like to swoon
A Diana, from her troubled draperies
In carved escape, a slim arrested moon

Across the tangled yew she has for screen
Gazes on the stagnant lilied green
Of water, there another face to see
That, like hers, upon it loves to lean.

As autumn and the moon of death draw nigh
The sad long days of summer herein lie;
And she, too, warm in sorrow, 'neath the trees
Turns to night, and weeps, and longs to die.

Above the chesnut trees and bloom-starred ground
The moon flies up the sky without a sound,
And by the leaves snared like a silver bird,
Sleeps in the lilies like a maiden drowned.

Ah, Spring, that with nightingale and rose
Pillages and sacks this ancient close,
And puts to sweet soft sword the citadel,
And then before the summer onward goes;

If like this drowning moon I could remain
Forever locked in sleep, when spring again
Returns to storm these ancient walls, and look
To find me here, then it would look in vain.

O let me be, too deep to stir and wake
'Neath all a summer's sleep is short to slake,
As this dead pool, when there have died away
The ripples under which a heart did break.

William Faulkner.

Figure 5.   Typescript of "Adolescence" (#2b)
*(Courtesy Jill Faulkner Summers and the William Faulkner
Collection, University of Virginia Library)*

a. "L'Apres-Midi d'un Faune," 1 p. typescript on back of J. W. T. Falkner's First National Bank stationery: 32 lines in 2 verses; first line "I peep through slender trees"; below typed poem are 13 penciled holograph lines also from this poem; this is the earliest version of the poem; ViU (Accession #9817-b).

b. Untitled, 1 p. penciled holograph manuscript: 40 lines in 2 strophes, 6+ lines canceled; first line "I follow her through singing trees"; ViU (Accession #9817-b).

c. Untitled, 1 p. penciled holograph manuscript: 41 lines in 2 strophes, 5 partially canceled; first line "I follow through the singing trees"; ViU (Accession #9817-b).

d. Untitled, 1 p. penciled holograph fragment on torn piece of lined paper: 10 lines; first line "Shakes down her blown and vagrant hair"; author's illustration to right of poem; on other side is fragment from "A Dead Dancer" (#24d); ViU (Accession #9817-b).

e. "L'Apres-Midi [d'un Faune?]" 3 pp. holograph manuscript: burned fragments, parts of 40 lines visible; this is *The Lilacs* VI; *H/B 1982:* 26, pp. 21–23.

f. Untitled, penciled holograph fragment on torn half-cover of *Saturday Evening Post* 31 August 1918: 15 lines; first line "Ah, I peep through the trees"; *H/B 1982:* 24.

g. Untitled, penciled 4-line fragment below drafts of "A Dead Dancer" (#24f); first line "I have a sudden wish to go"; on other side is penciled fragment of "The Ace" (#1b); ViU (Accession #9817-b).

8. "April" [*PV:6]

Con 1 (1 February 1932): 2; republished in *Lillabulero:* 24. *VIS:* 86–88.

a. "April," 3 pp. photocopy of carbon typescript: 40 lines; "86," "87," and "88" typed at bottom of each consecutive page; below "88" on the final page is typed "(end)."; this is *Vision in Spring* XIV; ViU (Accession #9817-I).

b. "April," 2 pp. black ribbon typescript on legal-size paper: 4 ten-line strophes; above title is penciled "9"; this is included in [*Virginia 3*] (#172); ViU (Accession #6074).

c. Untitled, 2 pp. black ribbon typescript: burned fragment, 32 lines visible, 27 complete; first visible phrase "Clad in its own [?]"; "William Faulkner" typed at bottom; type and paper indicate that these are 2 leaves of the same typescript; TxU.

9. "Aubade. Provence. Sixth Century"

Transcribed in *Man Collecting:* 125–26.

 a. "Aubade. Provence. Sixth Century," 1 p. purple ribbon typescript on legal-size paper: 4 stanzas, 32 lines; ViU (Accession #6271-AK).

10. "Une Ballade des Femmes Perdues" [*PV:8]

Mis 28 January 1920: 3 and *EPP:* 54.

 a. "Une Ballade des Femmes Perdues," 2 pp. holograph manuscript: parts of 19 lines visible; this is *The Lilacs* VII; *H/B 1982:* 26, pp. 24–25.

11. ["Behind the mask—a maiden's face"]

Transcribed in *Bonner:* 3.

 a. Untitled, 1 p. penciled holograph manuscript on lined paper: 10 lines; paper folder for poem reads "Poem / inside" followed by first and second line; LNT.

12. ["Below the misted rainbow falls"]

Manuscript of this fragment reproduced in *Gifts:* plate 2.

 a. Untitled, 1 p. ribbon typescript: burned fragment, 27 lines visible, 21 complete; 2 holograph corrections, apparently in Faulkner's hand; *H/B 1982:* 27a.

13. "Bill"

HC/MP: 112; the manuscript is reproduced in *HC 1981:* n.p. The only extant manuscript is *Helen: A Courtship* (#163), dated "PASCA-GOULA-JUNE-1925"; LNT.

14. ["The black bird swung in the white rose tree"] [*UF:11]

Typescript (a) reproduced in *Selections:* figure 10.

 a. Untitled, 1 p. purple ribbon typescript: 21 lines, 3 stanzas; this is included in the [*Aunt Bama Poems*], though not in the numbered sequence; *H/B 1982:* 18h; also available on aperture cards at ViU (Accession #6074, series VIII, box 11, #20).
 b. Untitled, 1 p. purple ribbon typescript: burned fragment, 17 lines visible, 14 complete; TxU.

c. Untitled, 1 p. typescript cut off at bottom: burned fragment, 3 seven-line stanzas, all complete except last 3 lines of last stanza; "XIII" above first line; apparently complete since "XIV" (number only, no lines) follows on same page; MsU (Wynn, folder 2, #14).

15. ["Bonny earth and bonny sky"] [*PV:9]

This is *AGB* XV: 36, which survives only in setting copy, galley proofs, and printed text. See *A Green Bough* (#162) for manuscript information.

16. "Cathay" [*PV:10]

Mis 12 November 1919: 8 and *EPP:* 41. Typescript (a) reproduced in *Meriwether:* figure 3. The poem is quoted and discussed in Richardson 1969.

a. "Cathay," 1 p. black ribbon typescript: 2 stanzas, 20 lines; text differs slightly from *Mis* version; ViU (Accession #6074).
b. "Cathay," 1 p. purple carbon typescript: burned fragment, 20 lines visible, 16 complete; TxU.
c. "Cathay," 2 pp. manuscript: burned fragments, 20 lines visible, none complete; this is *The Lilacs* II; *H/B 1982:* 26, pp. 15–16.

17. "A Child Looks from his Window" [*PV:11]

Con 2 (25 May 1932): 3. *Lillabulero:* 29. Titled "If Cats Could Fly," the same poem appears in *Blotner 1974:* 399.

a. "A Child Looks from his Window," 1 p. black ribbon typescript: 16 lines; ViU (Accession #6074).
b. "If Cats could Fly," 1 p. black ribbon typescript: burned fragment, 13 lines visible, 10 complete; ink holograph "[?] for children." at top; author's illustration to right of poem; TxU.

18. "Clair de Lune" [*PV:12]

Mis 3 March 1920: 6 and *EPP:* 58. Polk 1977 reprints the poem in his introduction to *TM:* xii. The poem is also quoted and compared to Verlaine's poem of the same name in Samway 1982 and quoted and discussed in Marshall 1987. No known extant manuscripts or typescripts.

19. "A Clymène" [*PV:1]

Mis 14 April 1920: 3 and *EPP:* 61. No known extant manuscripts or typescripts.

20. "Co-education at Ole Miss" [*PV:14]

Mis 4 May 1921: 5 and *EPP:* 77. No known extant manuscripts or typescripts.

21. "The Dancer"

VIS: 65–66. Quoted and compared to Conrad Aiken's "Dancing Adairs" in *Origins:* 186–87.

a. "The Dancer," 2 pp. photocopy of carbon typescript: 20 lines; at bottoms of pages are consecutive numbers "65" and "66"; this is *Vision in Spring* X; ViU (Accession #9817-I).

b. "The Dancer," 1 p. purple ribbon typescript: 20 lines in quatrains; above the title, in ink, is the number "1"; beneath the title is typed "to V. de G. F." (Faulkner's stepdaughter); first line "I am Youth, so white, so slim"; at bottom the number "4," in parentheses, has been erased, but is still legible; also at bottom in pencil are circled "1" and "2"; this is included in [*Virginia 1*] (#170); ViU (Accession #6074).

22. ["The dark ascends"] [*UF:18]

VIS: 36–39. Second leaf of typescript (c) reproduced in *VIS:* Appendix B (p. xliii). Note: also untitled, *VIS* VII has identical first line—see "A Symphony" (#107) for further information about *VIS* VII.

a. Untitled, 4 pp. photocopy of carbon typescript: 47 lines; at bottom of each page are consecutive numbers "36," "37," "38," and "39"; this is *Vision in Spring* VI; ViU (Accession #9817-I).

b. Untitled, 2 pp. black ribbon typescript: burned fragment, 41 lines visible, 31 complete; first line "The dark ascends"; black ink holograph "6." above poem; pinholes in the upper left corner and type indicate that these 2 leaves form 1 typescript; TxU.

c. Untitled, 2 pp. black ribbon typescript: burned fragment, 38 lines visible, 19 complete; first visible phrase "spun between the darkening ends of walls"; at end is typed "William Faulkner. / July 1920."; appears to be earliest extant version of *VIS* VI; TxU.

23. "Dawn"

Photocopy (a) reproduced in *Stylization:* 87 (figures 83–85).

a. "Dawn," 1 p. photocopy of holograph manuscript: 8 lines; this is one of the [*Estelle Poems*] (#161); location of original unknown; photocopy ViU (Accession #9817-I).

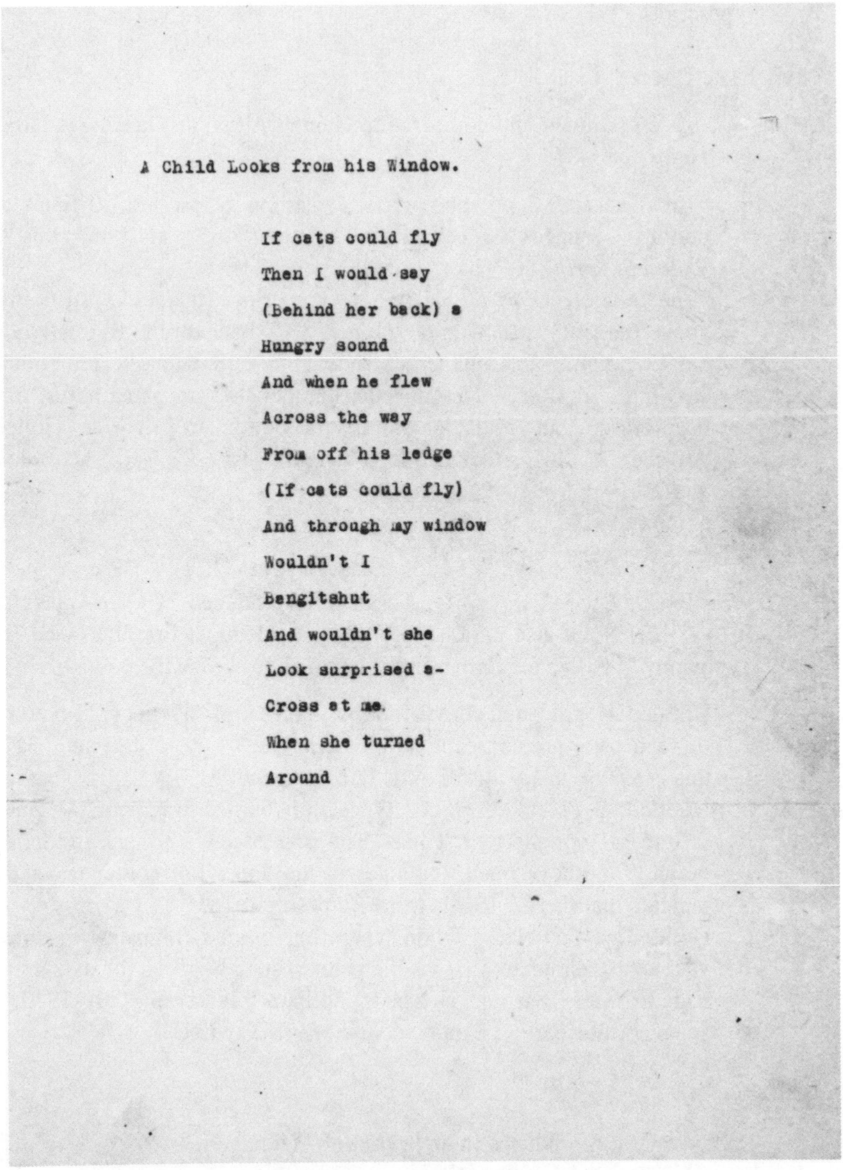

A Child Looks from his Window.

If cats could fly
Then I would say
(behind her back) a
Hungry sound
And when he flew
Across the way
From off his ledge
(If cats could fly)
And through my window
Wouldn't I
bangitshut
And wouldn't she
Look surprised a-
Cross at me.
When she turned
Around

Figure 6. Typescript of "A Child Looks from his Window" (#17a)
*(Courtesy Jill Faulkner Summers and the William Faulkner
Collection, University of Virginia Library)*

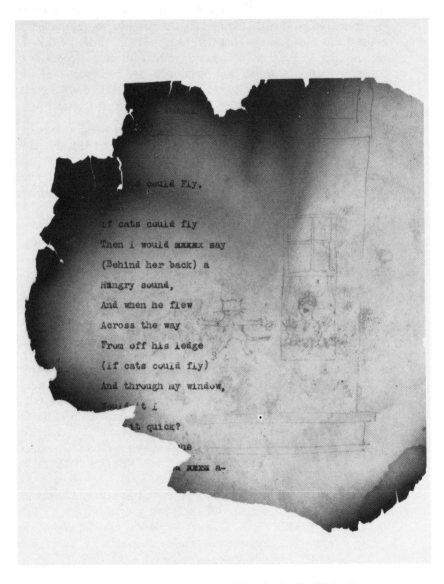

Figure 7.   Burned Typescript of "A Child Looks from his Window"
("If Cats could Fly") with Faulkner's Own Illustration (#17b)
*(Courtesy Jill Faulkner Summers and the Harry Ransom
Humanities Research Center, The University of Texas, Austin)*

24. "A Dead Dancer" [*UF:58]

Manuscript (b) reproduced in *Man Collecting:* 124. Manuscripts (e) and (f) transcribed in *Man Collecting:* 128–29. Manuscripts (a) through (c) collated and transcribed in *Man Collecting:* 131–33. L. D. Brodsky has reconstructed and collated *The Lilacs* version (d) of this poem to the collation in *Man Collecting* and published it and 3 fragments of other versions (e–g) in Brodsky 1981. Manuscript (e) reproduced in *Gifts:* plate 1. 1 page of manuscript (g) reproduced in *Stylization:* 28 (figure 20).

a. "A Dead Dancer," 1 p. ink holograph manuscript on legal-size paper: 40 lines, 4 strophes, 4 1/2 lines canceled; on other side is (b) below; ViU (Accession #9817-b).
b. Untitled, 1 p. penciled holograph manuscript: 43 lines, 5 strophes, 4+ lines canceled; first line "We, that she had loved at different times"; on other side is (a) above; ViU (Accession #9817-b).
c. "A Dead Dancer," 1 p. ink holograph manuscript on other side of M. C. Falkner Hardware Store stationery: 26 lines, 3 strophes, 3 words canceled; ViU (Accession #9817-b).
d. Untitled, 1 p. penciled holograph manuscript: burned fragment, 3 lines; first visible phrase "girl she is dead"; on other side is fragment of "L'Apres-Midi d'un Faun" (#7d); ViU (Accession #9817-b).
e. Untitled, 1 p. penciled holograph manuscript on lined paper: 15 lines; first line "This girl she is dead"; appears to be an early version of (a) above; ViU (Accession #9817-b).
f. Untitled, 1 p. penciled holograph manuscript: 18 lines, 3 canceled; first line "This girl, she is dead, is dead"; at bottom of page is a fragment from "L'Apres-Midi d'un Faune" (#7g); on other side is penciled fragment of "The Ace" (#1b); this is three drafts of the first strophe of the poem; ViU (Accession #9817-b).
g. "A Dead Dancer," 3 pp. ink holograph manuscript: burned fragment, parts of 27 lines visible; this is *The Lilacs* XII; *H/B 1982:* 26, pp. 31–33.
h. Untitled, ink holograph manuscript: burned fragment, 22 lines in 2 strophes, 2 lines canceled; *H/B 1982:* 23a.
i. Untitled, Brodsky "Dead Dancer" fragments. Like all unpublished items in the Brodsky collection, these manuscripts are not available to the public. For Brodsky's descriptions, see *H/B 1982:* 23b-d.

25.   "A Dead Pilot" [*PV:15]

AGB XVIII: 40. *James:* 34 (titled "Boy and Eagle").

a.   "A Dead Pilot," 1 p. black ribbon typescript: 21 lines; at upper left is typed "William Faulkner / Oxford, Miss"; TxU.

b.   "A Dead Pilot," 1 p. carbon typescript of (a) above; TxU.

c.   "[?] Aeroplane," 1 p. black carbon typescript: burned fragment, parts of 16 lines and title visible; TxU.

d.   "A Dead Pilot," 1 p. black ribbon typescript: 21 lines, all complete; "William Faulkner / Oxford, Miss" typed in upper left corner beside title; TxU.

26.   "December: / To Elise." [*UV:34]

HC/MP: 157. Typescript (a) reproduced in *MP 1979:* 37.

a.   "December: / To Elise," 1 p. carbon typescript: 16 lines, 4 quatrains; at bottom is typed "William Faulkner" and "Oxford, Mississippi, /December 15, 1924"; holograph signature; this is one of the unsequenced *Mississippi Poems, H/B 1982:* 45k.

b.   "To Elise," 1 p. black ribbon typescript on legal-size paper: 4 quatrains; at top in ink is written, not in Faulkner's hand, *"Dedication";* at bottom is typed "5 December, 1924"; although unnumbered, this is included in [*Virginia 3*] (#172); ViU (Accession #6074).

c.   Untitled, 1 p. black ribbon typescript: burned fragment, parts of 6 lines visible; first visible phrase "your flesh; but now is dull"; TxU.

27.   "Drowning" [*PV:16]

AGB XIX: 41. *James:* 32 (titled "Green is the Water" and divided into 2 verses, one of 4 lines and one of 8).

a.   "Drowning," 1 p. typescript: 16 lines in quatrains; dated in ink holograph "2 April 25"; this version has a second stanza that does not appear in *AGB;* NN-B.

b.   "Drowning," 1 p. typescript: 15 lines, first 4 and last 8 in quatrains; an earlier draft of (a); NN-B.

c.   "Drowning," 1 p. black ribbon typescript: burned fragment, 12 lines visible, 5 complete; TxU.

d.   "Drowning," 1 p. typescript: burned fragment, 16 lines visible, 8 complete, 1 canceled; TxU.

28. "Dying Gladiator" [*PV:17]

   DD 7 (January-February 1925): 85, *EPP:* 113, and *Salmagundi:* 43–44.

   a. Untitled, 1 p. purple ribbon typescript: burned fragment, parts of 11 lines visible; "[Faulkn?]er" typed at bottom of page; TxU.
   b. Untitled, 1 p. purple ribbon typescript: burned fragment, 14 lines visible, 10 complete; first visible phrase "torches were less, and trumpets aloft in the portals"; "William Faulkner." typed at bottom; TxU.
   c. "Dying Gladiator," 1 p. typescript: burned fragment, 20 lines visible, 18 complete; "2" and "3" circled in pencil at bottom; variant of *DD* version; MsU (Wynn, folder 8, #44).

29. "Elder Watson in Heaven" [*UV:11]

   Transcribed in Brodsky 1985.

   a. "Elder Watson in Heaven," 2 pp. typescript: 9 quatrains; this is one of Brodsky's unnumbered [*Aunt Bama Poems*]; *HB 1982:* 18k; ViU aperture cards (Accession #6074, box 11, #20).

30. "Eros" [*PV:18]

   AGB XXV: 47. This title is given only in a typescript setting copy of *AGB*.

   a. Untitled, 1 p. black ribbon typescript: burned fragment, 16 lines visible, 8 complete; first visible phrase "this a dream?"; TxU.
   b. Untitled, 1 p. black ribbon typescript: burned fragment, 20 lines visible, 4 complete; first visible phrase "[see?]med I lay"; TxU.

31. "Eros After" [*PV:19]

   AGB XXVI: 48.

   a. "Eros After," 1 p. black ribbon typescript: burned sheet but all 9 lines of poem complete; TxU.
   b. "And After," 1 p. typescript: burned sheet but the 9-line poem is complete except for the initial letter of first line; TxU.

32. "Estelle" [*UV: 12]

Transcribed and compared to James Joyce's "Villanelle of the Temptress" in *Stylization:* 111.

   a. "Estelle," 1 p. black ribbon typescript: burned, but the 11-line poem is complete; 1 holograph correction; TxU.
   b. Untitled, 1 p. black ribbon typescript: burned fragment, 11 lines visible, 8 complete; first visible line "Ah, and [sweet her mou?]th, and cold"; TxU.

33. "Eunice" [*UV:13]

Transcribed in Brodsky 1978.

   a. "Eunice," 3 pp. typescript: 68 lines in quatrains; this is one of the unsequenced [*Aunt Bama Poems*]; *H/B 1982:* 18j; aperture cards at ViU (Accession #6074, box 11, #20).
   b. "Eunice," 3 pp. purple ribbon typescript on legal-size paper: 17 quatrains; several pencil holograph corrections on last page; "William Faulkner" typed on all pages bottom left; the bottoms of the three pages are numbered consecutively "(17)," "(18)," and "(19)"; these numbers have been erased but are legible; although unnumbered, this poem is included in [*Virginia 1*] (#170); ViU (Accession #6074).
   c. Untitled, 1 p. carbon typescript: burned fragment, 15 lines visible, 10 complete; first visible phrase "like her"; TxU.
   d. Untitled, 5 severely damaged fragments containing phrases identifiable as "Eunice"; TxU.

34. "Fantouches" [*PV:20]

Mis 25 February 1920: 3. *EPP:* 57 (titled "Fantoches"). No known extant manuscripts or typescripts.

35. "The Faun" [*PV:21]

DD 7 (April 1925): 148. *New Orleans Item* 29 August 1954: 1, 18. *EPP:* 19. *Salamagundi:* 42. *HC/MP:* 114; manuscript (c) reproduced in *HC 1981:* n.p.

   a. "The Faun," 1 p. typescript: 14 lines; variant first line "When April like a Faun whose stampings ring"; "William Faulkner" typed at bottom left; MsU (Rowan Oak, box 2, folder 27).

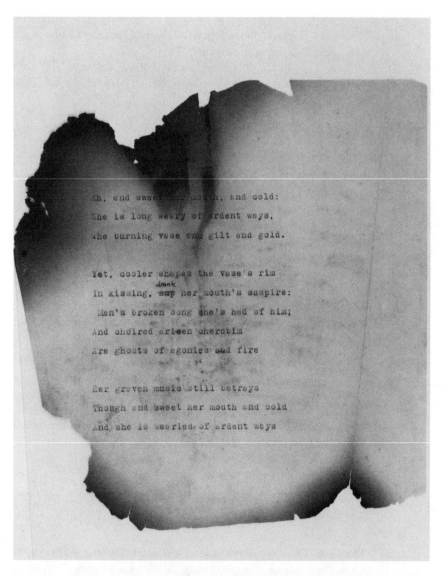

Figure 8.   Burned but Complete Typescript of "Estelle" (#32a)
*(Courtesy Jill Faulkner Summers and the Harry Ransom
Humanities Research Center, The University of Texas, Austin)*

b. "The Faun," 1 p. carbon typescript: burned fragment, 14 lines visible, 12 complete; below title is typed dedication "To H. L." (Harold Levy—see Collins 1981); TxU.

c. Untitled, 1 p. ink holograph manuscript: sonnet; this is *Helen: A Courtship* III, dated "PASCAGOULA-JUNE-1925"; LNT.

36. "The Flowers That Died" [*PV:22]

Con 3 (25 June 1933): 1.

a. Untitled, 1 p. black ribbon typescript on legal-size paper: 5 quatrains, 1 ink holograph revision; first line "The flowers that died last year again are growing"; title in pencil (not in Faulkner's hand) erased but legible; "2." typed above first line; text identical to *Con* version; this is included in [*Virginia 2*] (#171); ViU (Accession #6074).

b. Untitled, 1 p. black carbon typescript: burned fragment, 16 lines visible, 10 complete; first line "The flowers that died last year again are growing"; TxU.

c. Untitled, 5 burned carbon typescripts in various stages of disintegration; TxU.

37. "Floyd Collins" [*PV:23]

AGB III: 16–19.

a. "Floyd Collins," 5 pp. typescript: 92 lines, 3 cancelations; page numbers at bottoms of pages; MsU (Rowan Oak, box 2, folder 26).

b. "The Cave," 4 pp. carbon typescript: 93 lines, all complete; "William Faulkner / Oxford, Miss." typed at bottom of each page; TxU.

c. Untitled, 1 p. black ribbon typescript: burned fragment, 15 lines visible, 12 complete; first visible phrase "the music flies"; "William Faulkner / Oxford Miss" typed at bottom; "December 1924" in ink holograph below; TxU.

d. Untitled, 1 p. black ribbon typescript: burned fragment, 21 lines visible, 13 complete; first visible phrase "Then seven lights"; TxU.

e. Untitled, 1 p. typescript: burned fragment, 21 lines visible, 7 complete; first visible phrase "still unconquered"; TxU.

f. Untitled, 1 p. black ribbon typescript: severely burned fragment, 17 lines visible, 4 complete; first visible phrase "rumored far"; TxU.

g. Untitled, 1 p. typescript: burned fragment, 22 lines visible, 7 complete; first visible phrase "to bough"; TxU.

h. Untitled, 1 p. black ribbon typescript: burned fragment, parts of 7 lines visible; first visible word "mace"; TxU.

    i.   Untitled, 1 p. black ribbon typescript: burned fragment, 22 lines visible, 14 complete; first visible phrase "spears of starlight"; TxU.

    j.   Untitled, 1 p. black ribbon typescript: burned fragment, 21 lines visible, 8 complete; first visible phrase "[slu?]mber seeks"; TxU.

    k.   Untitled, 1 p. black ribbon typescript: burned fragment, 23 lines visible, 13 complete; first visible phrase "golen (*canc.*) hair" ("golen" is corrected in ink holograph to "golden"); TxU.

38.   "The Gallows" [*PV:24]

AGB XIV: 34–35. *HC/MP:* 160. Typescript (g) reproduced in *MP 1979:* 31.

    a.   "The Gallows," 1 p. typescript: 20 lines, all complete; TxU.

    b.   "The Gallows," 1 p. black ribbon typescript: burned fragment, 18 lines visible, 13 complete; TxU.

    c.   "The Gallows," 1 p. black ribbon typescript: burned fragment, 13 lines visible, 8 complete; TxU.

    d.   "[The G?]allows," 1 p. black ribbon typescript: burned fragment, 19 lines visible, 14 complete; TxU.

    e.   Untitled, 1 p. black ribbon typescript: burned fragment, 16 lines visible, 13 complete; first visible phrase "[c?]alled him felon"; fourth quatrain canceled in pencil; TxU.

    f.   "The Gallows," 1 p. carbon typescript: burned fragment, 19 lines visible, 16 complete; TxU.

    g.   "The Gallows," 1 p. carbon typescript: 20 lines, all complete; typed at bottom of page, "William Faulkner, / Oxford, Mississippi, / 29 Oct. 1924"; signed in holograph below dateline, "William Faulkner"; 3 substantive variants from *AGB* XIV; this is one of Brodsky's unnumbered *Mississippi Poems; H/B 1982:* 45h.

    h.   "The Gallows," 1 p. ribbon typescript: 3 stanzas, 20 lines, all complete; signed in ink holograph, "William Faulkner / Oxford / 29 October 1924"; this is one of the Wynn *Mississippi Poems;* MsU (Wynn, folder 6, #31).

    i.   Untitled, 1 p. black ink holograph manuscript: burned fragment; contains 3 drafts of first stanza, 2 drafts of second stanza, 1 draft of third stanza; first line in all three versions "His mother said I'll make him"; on other side is holograph draft of poem fragment beginning "[?] he gaped and cried" (#188); MsU (Wynn, folder 9).

39. ["Goodbye, goodnight: goodnight were more than fair"]

MP/HC: 120. Manuscript reproduced in *HC 1981:* n.p. This is *Helen: A Courtship* IX, dated "GENOA-AUGUST-1925," the only known extant manuscript of the poem (see #163); LNT.

40. ["Green grow the rushes O"]

Transcribed in *Selections:* 26.

  a. Untitled, purple ribbon typescript: two quatrains; this is [*Aunt Bama Poems*] VII; *H/B 1982:* 18g and aperture cards ViU (Accession #6074, box 11, #20).

41. "Guidebook" [*PV:26]

AGB IV: 20–21. 5 lines with several differences from the *AGB* version appear in *Mosquitoes:* 249.

  a. "Guidebook," 1 p. black ribbon typescript: burned fragment, 14 lines visible, 12 complete; at top left is typed "[Will?]iam Faulkner /[Rue?] Servandoni"; TxU.
  b. "Guidebook," 1 p. black ribbon typescript: burned fragment, 16 lines visible, 10 complete; at top left is typed "[?] Faulkner / [?] Miss."; TxU.
  c. "guidebook," 1 p. black ribbon typescript: burned fragment, 17 lines visible, 13 complete; at top left is typed "[?] Faulkner / [?] Miss."; TxU.
  d. Untitled, 1 p. black ribbon typescript: burned fragment, 16 lines visible, 10 complete; first visible phrase "his brilliant counterattack saying"; TxU.
  e. Untitled, 1 p. black ribbon typescript: burned fragment, 18 lines visible, 4 complete; first visible phrase ''[bri?]lliant counterattack saying"; TxU.
  f. Untitled, 1 p. black ribbon typescript: burned fragment, 18 lines visible, 14 complete; first visible line "shhhhhhh to general blah in the year mille"; TxU.
  g. Untitled, 1 p. black ribbon typescript: burned fragment, parts of 5 lines visible; first visible phrase "sleeps quietly decay"; at bottom left is typed "Paris / 27 Aug 1925"; TxU.
  h. Untitled, 1 p. black ribbon typescript: burned fragment, last 5 lines of poem visible, 1 complete; first visible phrase "in lanes he"; TxU.
  i. Untitled, 1 p. black ribbon typescript: burned fragment, last 4 lines of poem complete; first visible phrase "sleeps quietly decay"; TxU.

The Gallows.

His mother said: I'll make him
A lad as ne'er has been
(And rocked him closely, stroking
His soft hair's golden sheen)
His bright youth will be metal
No alchemist has seen.

His mother said: I'll give him
A bright and high desire
'Till all the dross of living
Burns clean within his fire.
He'll be strong and merry
And he'll be clean and brave,
And all the worldwill rue it
When he is dark in grave.

But dark will treat him kinder
Than man would anywhere
(With barren winds to rock him
---Though now he doesn't care---
And hushèd and haughty starlight
To stroke his golden hair)

Figure 9.   Complete Typescript of "The Gallows" (#38a)
(Courtesy Jill Faulkner Summers and the Harry Ransom
Humanities Research Center, The University of Texas, Austin)

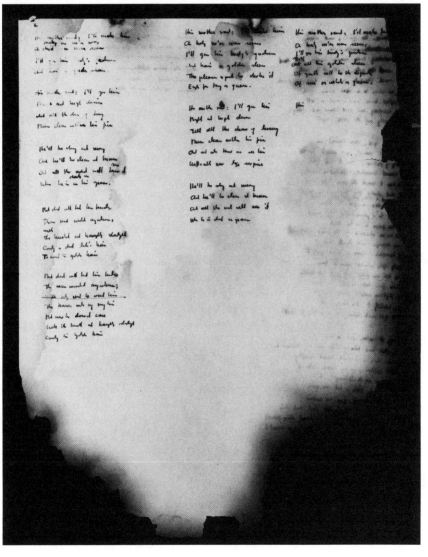

Figure 10.   Holograph Drafts of "The Gallows" (#38i)
(Courtesy Jill Faulkner Summers and the University of Mississippi Library)

j. Untitled, *Mosquitoes* typescript, ff. 332–33: 5 lines; first line "O spring o wanton o cruel"; this version has several minor differences from the published *Mosquitoes* version of the poem; ViU.

42. "Hank Cadwalader"

Transcribed in *Man Collecting:* 130.

a. "Hank Cadwalader," 1 p. black ribbon typescript: 7 four-line strophes; ViU (Accession #9817-b).

43. ["He furrows the brown earth, doubly sweet"] [*PV:27 and *UF:28]

AGB VIII: 27–28. *HC/MP:* 153–54. Typescript (c) reproduced in *MP 1979:* 21, 23.

a. Untitled, 1 p. black ribbon typescript: burned fragment, 13 lines visible, 11 complete; first visible line "Inscribes the answer to its life"; TxU.
b. Untitled, 1 p. black ribbon typescript: burned fragment, parts of first 3 quatrains visible, 8 lines complete; TxU.
c. Untitled, 2 pp. typescript: 8 quatrains; the first line is identical to that in manuscript (b) above, but (c) contains substantive variants throughout, variants suggesting that (c) is an earlier draft of (b); this is Brodsky's *Mississippi Poems* V; *H/B 1982:* 45e.
d. Untitled, 2 pp. ribbon typescript: 8 quatrains; identical to (c) above except for 1 accidental; "William Faulkner" typed at bottom; this is Wynn *Mississippi Poems* V; MsU (Wynn, folder 7, #37–38).
e. Untitled, 2 pp. typescript: first page is a burned fragment, 23 lines visible, 20 complete; second page contains 2 quatrains; holograph "1" circled in left margin below poem and above poem II; this is first poem of *Michael* with "Michael" typed above Roman numeral I; "Taken out and [?] moved [?] Mississ[ippi?] Poe[ms?]" written next to title in unidentified hand; MsU (Wynn, folder 1, #1–2).

44. "Helen and the Centaur" [*UV:15]

HC/MP: 118. Manuscript (a) reproduced in *HC 1981:* n.p.

a. Untitled, 1 p. holograph manuscript: sonnet; dated "PASCAGOULA-JUNE-1925"; this is *Helen: A Courtship* VII; LNT.
b. "Helen and the Centaur," 1 p. black ribbon typescript: burned fragment, sonnet with all 14 lines complete; final 3 lines canceled and heavily revised in black ink holograph; black ink holograph dateline "[Pascago?]ula, Miss" at bottom; this is an earlier version of *HC* VII

with lines 8 and 12 through 14 substantially different from published version; TxU.

45. "Hermaphroditus" [*PV:28]

   AGB XXXVIII: 61. *Mosquitoes:* 252. Quoted and discussed as reworking of Swinburne in Kreisworth 1983: 7–10.

   a. "Hermaphroditus," *Mosquitoes* typescript, p. 336: sonnet; holograph revisions; ViU.
   b. Untitled, 1 p. typescript: burned fragment, 14 lines visible, 11 complete; first visible phrase "that of thy weary all seem weariest"; 4 ink holograph revisions; TxU.
   c. "Hermaphroditus," 1 p. black ribbon typescript: sonnet with all 14 lines visible and complete; "Eva Wiseman / from 'Satyricon in Starlight'" typed at bottom right; note in black ink holograph at bottom reads "Can you send $10.00 or maybe $15.00, or perhaps $8.00 or $4.50? A circumspect man can buy it for $4.50. If you can't do more, send love and kind regards. With kindest personal regards I am and &etc."; 3 more lines canceled below; TxU (catalogued under "Faulkner W., Misc.—Wiseman / Eva, Hermaphroditus").

46. ["Her tears are what men call dew"]

   This burned typescript fragment is reproduced in *Gifts:* plate 3.

   a. Untitled, 1 p. ribbon typescript: burned fragment, 7 lines visible, 3 complete; typed below last line, "William Faulkner / April, 1920"; *H/B 1982:* 27c.

47. ["How canst thou be chaste, when lonely nights"] [*PV:29]

   AGB XXIV: 46. This poem survives only in setting copy, galley proof, and printed text. See manuscript entry for *AGB* (#162).

48. "The Husbandman" [*PV:7]

   AGB XXXI: 54. Additional stanza in (b) below printed in *Blotner 1974:* 1131.

   a. "Armistice," 1 p. black ribbon typescript: burned fragment, 12 lines visible, 10 complete; blue ink holograph revisions throughout; TxU.
   b. "The Husbandman," 1 p. typescript: 12 lines, all complete; subtitled "November 11, 1941" with pencil holograph correction to "1942"; 3 substantive variants from (a) in first stanza, third stanza added;

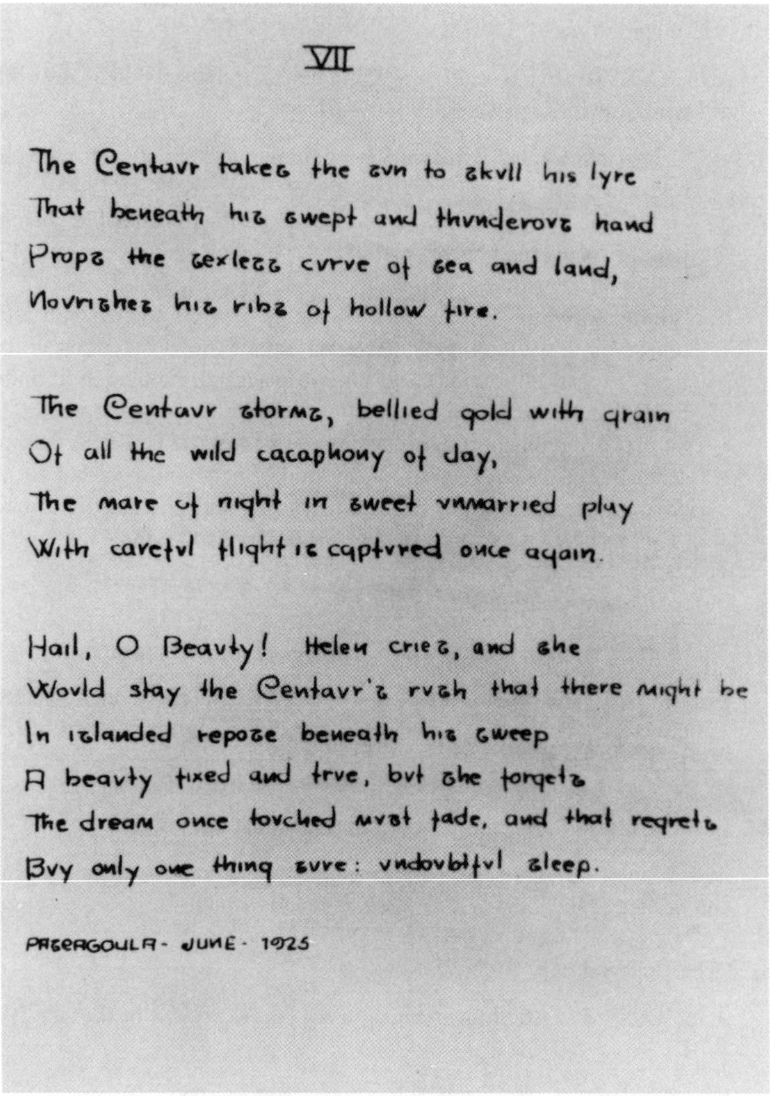

VII

The Centaur takes the sun to skull his lyre
That beneath his swept and thunderous hand
Props the sexless curve of sea and land,
Nourishes his ribs of hollow fire.

The Centaur storms, bellied gold with grain
Of all the wild cacophony of day,
The mare of night in sweet unmarried play
With careful flight is captured once again.

Hail, O Beauty! Helen cries, and she
Would stay the Centaur's rush that there might be
In islanded repose beneath his sweep
A beauty fixed and true, but she forgets
The dream once touched must fade, and that regrets
Buy only one thing sure: undoubtful sleep.

PASCAGOULA - JUNE - 1925

Figure 11. "Helen and the Centaur" (#44a)
From Faulkner's holograph sonnet sequence, *Helen: A Courtship.*
*(Courtesy Jill Faulkner Summers and the Howard-Tilton
Memorial Library, Tulane University)*

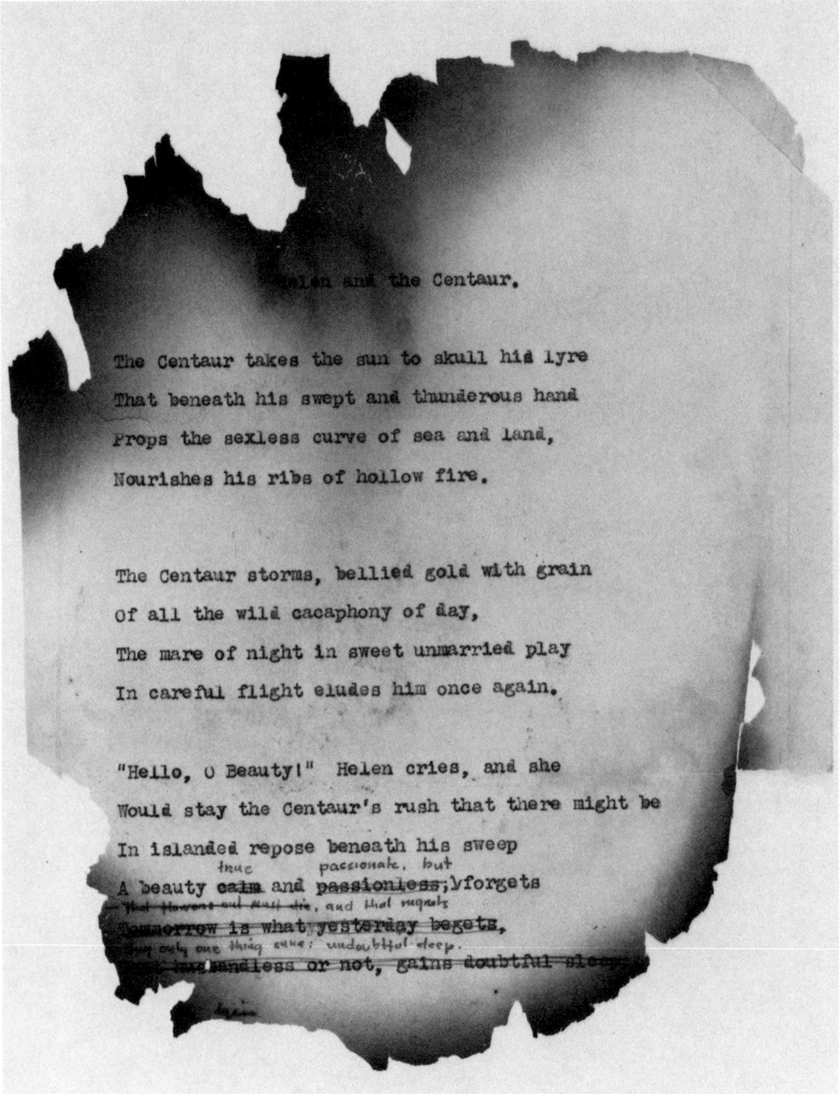

Helen and the Centaur.

The Centaur takes the sun to skull his lyre
That beneath his swept and thunderous hand
Props the sexless curve of sea and land,
Nourishes his ribs of hollow fire.

The Centaur storms, bellied gold with grain
Of all the wild cacaphony of day,
The mare of night in sweet unmarried play
In careful flight eludes him once again.

"Hello, O Beauty!" Helen cries, and she
Would stay the Centaur's rush that there might be
In islanded repose beneath his sweep
                      true   passionate, but
A beauty calm and passionless; forgets
    That flowers out must die, and that regrets
Tomorrow is what yesterday begets,
     And only one thing sure: undoubtful sleep.
        islandless or not, gains doubtful sleep

Figure 12.   Heavily Revised Typescript of "Helen and the Centaur" (#44b)
(Courtesy Jill Faulkner Summers and the Harry Ransom
Humanities Research Center, The University of Texas, Austin)

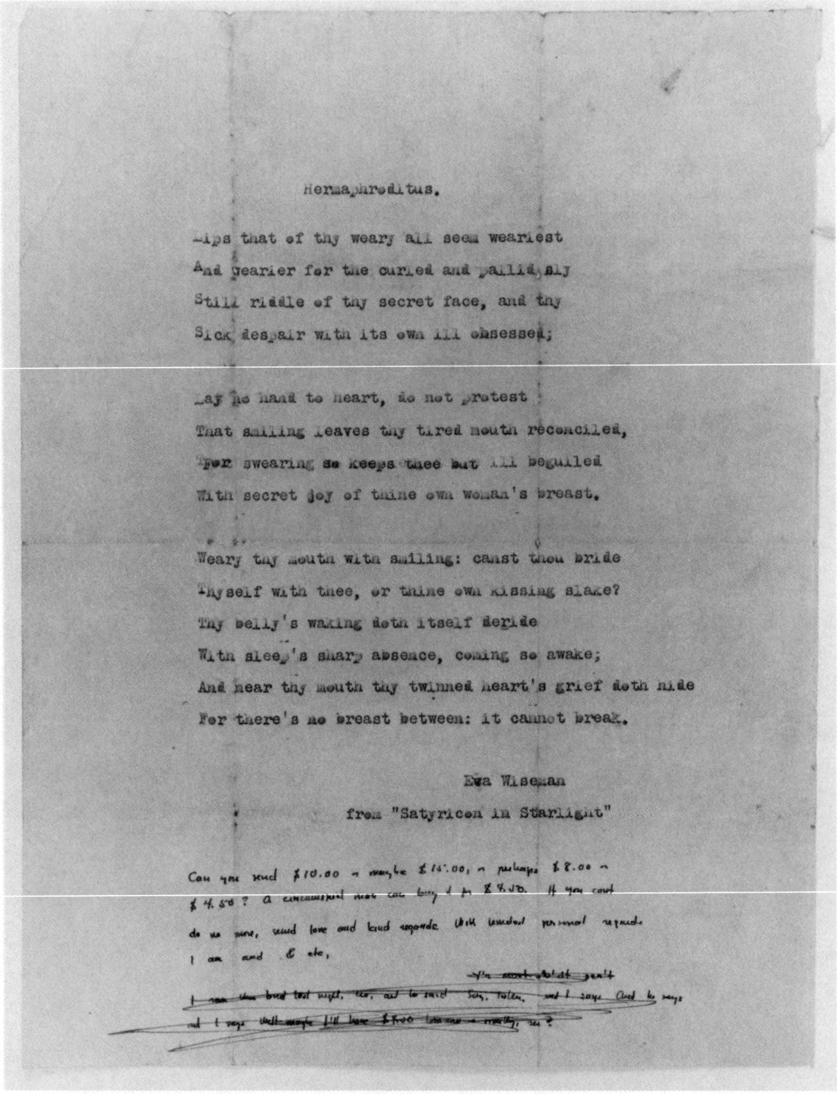

Hermaphroditus.

Lips that of thy weary all seem weariest
And wearier for the curled and pallid sly
Still riddle of thy secret face, and thy
Sick despair with its own ill obsessed;

Lay no hand to heart, do not protest
That smiling leaves thy tired mouth reconciled,
For swearing so keeps thee but ill beguiled
With secret joy of thine own woman's breast.

Weary thy mouth with smiling: canst thou bride
Thyself with thee, or thine own kissing slake?
Thy belly's waking doth itself deride
With sleep's sharp absence, coming so awake;
And near thy mouth thy twinned heart's grief doth hide
For there's no breast between: it cannot break.

Eva Wiseman
from "Satyricon in Starlight"

Figure 13. Typescript of "Hermaphroditus" by "Eva Wiseman"
with a Holograph Note from Her Author, William Faulkner (#45c)
(Courtesy Jill Faulkner Summers and the Harry Ransom
Humanities Research Center, The University of Texas, Austin)

"William Faulkner" typed at bottom right; this is *not* "November 11" (for *AGB* XXX, see #75); ViU (Accession #9817-b).

49. "Hymn"

Transcribed in *Man Collecting:* 126–27.

a. "Hymn," 2 pp. purple ribbon typescript on legal-size paper: 32 lines, 4 stanzas; contains 20 variants from (b) below, 9 substantive; ViU (Accession #6271-AK).
b. Untitled, 2 pp. typescript: burned fragment; first page has 24 lines visible, 23 complete; second page has 8 lines visible and complete; first line "Where shall we seek thee, O beauty? Aloft in the morning"; "William Faulkner" typed beneath last line but canceled; "2" and "3" circled in margin below; MsU (Wynn, folder 3, #15–16).

50. ["I give the world to love you"]

Transcribed in *Blotner 1974:* 185–86.

a. Untitled, 1 p. purple ribbon typescript: 3 quatrains; this is [*Aunt Bama Poems*] V; *H/B 1982:* 18e; aperture cards ViU (Accession #6074, box 11, #20).
b. Untitled, first 3 quatrains of [*Housman*], leaf C; "3" and "3" are circled in left margin with penciled remark, "Poor Shropshire Lad"; this is [*Housman*] X; MsU (Wynn, folder 2, #12).

51. ["I have seen music, heard"]

10-line poem quoted in *Wilde:* 76–77. No typescripts or manuscripts available, but the unpublished poem ["You have seen music, heard"] in the Wisdom Collection at LNT is remarkably similar (see #159).

52. ["I see your face through the twilight of my mind"] [*PV:31]

AGB XXII: 44. This poem survives only in setting copy, galley proof, and printed text. See listing for *A Green Bough* (#162).

53. "I Will Not Weep for Youth" [*PV:30]

Con 1 (1 February 1932): 1. Also appeared in *Wells:* 122 and *Lillabulero:* 28. Typescript (f) reproduced in *Perspective:* item 8.

a. Untitled, 1 p. typescript: 20 lines, 6 ink holograph revisions; first line "I will not weep for youth in after years"; the title appears to have been written in pencil in a hand not Faulkner's—though it has

THE HUSBANDMAN
November 11, 1941

He winnowed it with bayonets
And planted it with guns,
And when the final harrowing
Was healed by rains and suns

He looks about---and leaps to stamp
The stubborn grinning seeds
Of olden plantings back beneath
His field of colored weeds.

O flags, bloom out; blow out, bright flags.
The first wild bugle dies
Above seeds of old wars bared again
In lipless unsurprise.

                                    William Faulkner

Figure 14. Typescript of "The Husbandman," Datelined "November 11, 1942" (#48b)
            (Courtesy Jill Faulkner Summers and the William Faulkner
            Collection, University of Virginia Library)

been erased it is still faintly legible; below the title is typed Arabic numeral "1"; this is included in [*Virginia 2*] (#171); ViU (Accession #6074).

b. Untitled, 1 p. carbon typescript: burned fragment, 18 lines visible, 11 complete; first visible phrase "youth in after years"; Arabic numeral "1." typed center above first line; TxU.

c. Untitled, 1 p. typescript: burned fragment, parts of 15 lines visible; first visible phrase "with tears"; TxU.

d. Untitled, 1 p. carbon typescript: burned fragment, 17 lines visible in quatrains, 10 lines complete; first visible line "I do not weep for youth in after years"; TxU.

e. Untitled, 4 more severely burned carbon typescripts in various stages of disintegration; TxU.

f. "An Old Man Says," 1 p. purple ribbon typescript: 5 quatrains; this is included by Brodsky among the unsequenced [*Aunt Bama Poems*]; *H/B 1982:* 18i; aperture cards ViU (Accession #6074, box 11, #20).

54. "Indian Summer" [*PV:33]

AGB XXXV: 58. Published as "The Courtesan Is Dead" in *James:* 32. *HC/MP:* 151. Typescript (c) reproduced in *MP 1979:* 17.

a. "Indian Summer," 1 p. typescript: burned fragment, 14 lines visible, 10 complete; "3." typed above title; at bottom left is holograph dateline, "10 September 1924"; TxU.

b. "Indian Summer," 1 p. carbon typescript: burned, but poem is complete; this appears to be the carbon of (a) above; TxU.

c. "III / Indian Summer," 1 p. carbon typescript: 3 quatrains and a couplet; "William Faulkner" in typescript and holograph; this is Brodsky's *Mississippi Poems* III; *H/B 1982:* 45c.

d. "III / Indian Summer," 1 p. ribbon typescript: sonnet with all 14 lines complete; this is Wynn's *Mississippi Poems* III; MsU (Wynn, folder 7, #35).

55. "Interlude" [*UV:18]

VIS: 6–9. First page of fragment (c) reproduced in *VIS:* Appendix B (p. xl).

a. "Interlude," 4 pp. photocopy of carbon typescript: 49 lines; at bottoms of consecutive pages are numbers "6," "7," "8," and "9"; this is *Vision in Spring* II; ViU (Accession #9817-I).

    b. "Interlude," 3 pp. black ribbon typescript on legal-size paper; identical to *VIS* version except for some changes in accidentals; TxU.

    c. "Interlude," 2 pp. black ribbon typescript: burned fragment, 40 lines visible, 28 complete; black ink holograph "5." above title; TxU.

56. ["it matters not which one"]

Both sides of this leaf are reproduced in *Origins:* 111 and 113.

    a. Untitled, 1 p. purple ribbon typescript: burned fragment, 25 lines visible, 11 complete; on other side is a penciled holograph draft version of Faulkner's 1921 review of Conrad Aiken's *Turns and Movies* beginning "impersonality will never permit him to"; this is [*Texas*], leaf N (see #169); TxU.

57. "Knew I Love Once" [*PV:34]

Con 1 (1 February 1932): 1, *Wells:* 125, and *HC/MP:* 126. Faulkner changed the first line, deleted lines 5 through 8 of this sonnet, and made other substantive changes when he included it as *AGB* XXXIII: 56. Manuscript (e) reproduced in *HC 1981:* n.p. and in William Boozer's announcement article, *"Helen: A Courtship* Joins *Mayday* in Facsimile and Trade Editions." *The Faulkner Newsletter* 1.3 (July–September 1981): 1.

    a. Untitled, 1 p. black ribbon typescript: sonnet; first line "Knew I love once? Was it love or grief"; "William Faulkner" typed and canceled at bottom left; 2 holograph corrections; text, as corrected, identical to *Con* version; ViU (Accession #6074).

    b. Untitled, 1 p. typescript: sonnet; dated in ink holograph "25 March 25"; 4 lines that were dropped from the *AGB* version appear in this typescript; NN-B.

    c. Untitled, 1 p. ink holograph manuscript: 38 lines of trial and revision, beginning "Under the wild and bitter earth"; these lines are on the other side of the poem "Nostalgia" (see #142); NN-B.

    d. Untitled, 1 p. ink holograph manuscript: 29 lines of trial and revision, beginning "O mother sleep, when one by one these years"; NN-B.

    e. Untitled, 1 p. ink holograph manuscript: sonnet; dated "PARIS-SEP-TEMBER-1925"; this is *Helen: A Courtship* XV; LNT.

58. ["last beauty"]

First visible phrase of burned fragment. Manuscript (a) reproduced in *Selections:* 36 (figure 16), *Perspective:* item 14, and *H/B 1982:* 26 (figure

8). Typescript (b) reproduced in *Selections:* 37 (figure 16) and *H/B 1982:* 27 (figure 9).

    a.   Untitled, 1 p. penciled holograph manuscript: burned fragment, 20 lines visible, 1 canceled, 3 partially canceled, none complete; this is *[Texas]* (#169), leaf M; *H/B 1982:* 27h.

    b.   Untitled, 1 p. purple ribbon typescript: burned fragment, 23 lines, none complete; this is *[Texas]* (#169), leaf U; *H/B 1982:* 27g.

59. ["Lay me not the rose for lovers"] [*PV:35]

First of 4 lines quoted by A. Wigfall Green in "William Faulkner at Home," *SR* 40 (1932): 302. Green states that these lines are from a new collection of poems to be called *The Greening Bough.*

60. "Leaving Her" [*UV:note 2]

HC/MP: 124. Manuscript (a) reproduced in *HC 1981:* n.p. Manuscript (c) reproduced in Robert Wilson's *Modern Book Collecting* (New York: Knopf, 1980): 55.

    a.   Untitled, 1 p. holograph manuscript: sonnet; dated "LAGO MAG-GIORE-AUGUST-1925"; this is *Helen: A Courtship* XIII; LNT.

    b.   "Leaving Her," 1 p. ink holograph manuscript on legal-size paper: sonnet with 1 line canceled; McKeldin Library, MdU (see fig. 16).

    c.   "Leaving Her," "Obs[ession?] canceled, 1 p. ink holograph manuscript: 16 lines, parts of 7 canceled and revised; these lines followed by another draft of same poem: 19 lines, parts of 3 canceled; LDB.

    d.   "[Leav?]ing Her," 1 p. carbon typescript: burned fragment, 14 lines visible, 13 complete; extensive ink holograph revisions throughout; dated in ink holograph "[?]ber 1925" at bottom; TxU.

61. ["Let that sleep have no end, which brings me waking]

HC/MP: 122. Manuscript reproduced in *HC 1981:* n.p. This is *Helen: A Courtship* XI, dated "PAVIA-AUGUST-1925," the only known extant manuscript of the poem (see #163); LNT.

62. ["Let there be no farewell shaped between"]

HC/MP: 123. Manuscript reproduced in *HC 1981:* n.p. This is *Helen: A Courtship* XII; this manuscript, dated "LAGO MAGGIORE-AUGUST-

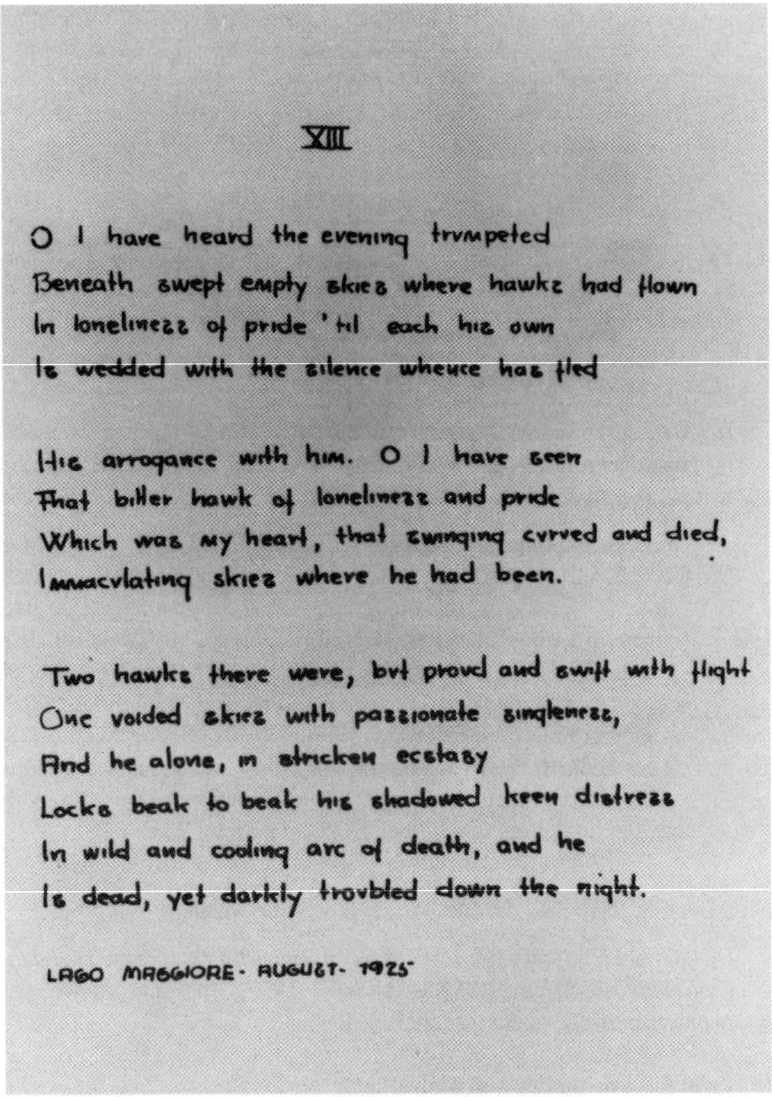

XIII

O I have heard the evening trumpeted
Beneath swept empty skies where hawks had flown
In loneliness of pride 'til each his own
Is wedded with the silence whence has fled

His arrogance with him. O I have seen
That bitter hawk of loneliness and pride
Which was my heart, that swinging curved and died,
Immaculating skies where he had been.

Two hawks there were, but proud and swift with flight
One voided skies with passionate singleness,
And he alone, in stricken ecstasy
Locks beak to beak his shadowed keen distress
In wild and cooling arc of death, and he
Is dead, yet darkly troubled down the night.

LAGO MAGGIORE · AUGUST · 1925

Figure 15. *Helen: A Courtship* XIII (#60a)
From the holograph sonnet sequence.
*(Courtesy Jill Faulkner Summers and the Howard-Tilton
Memorial Library, Tulane University)*

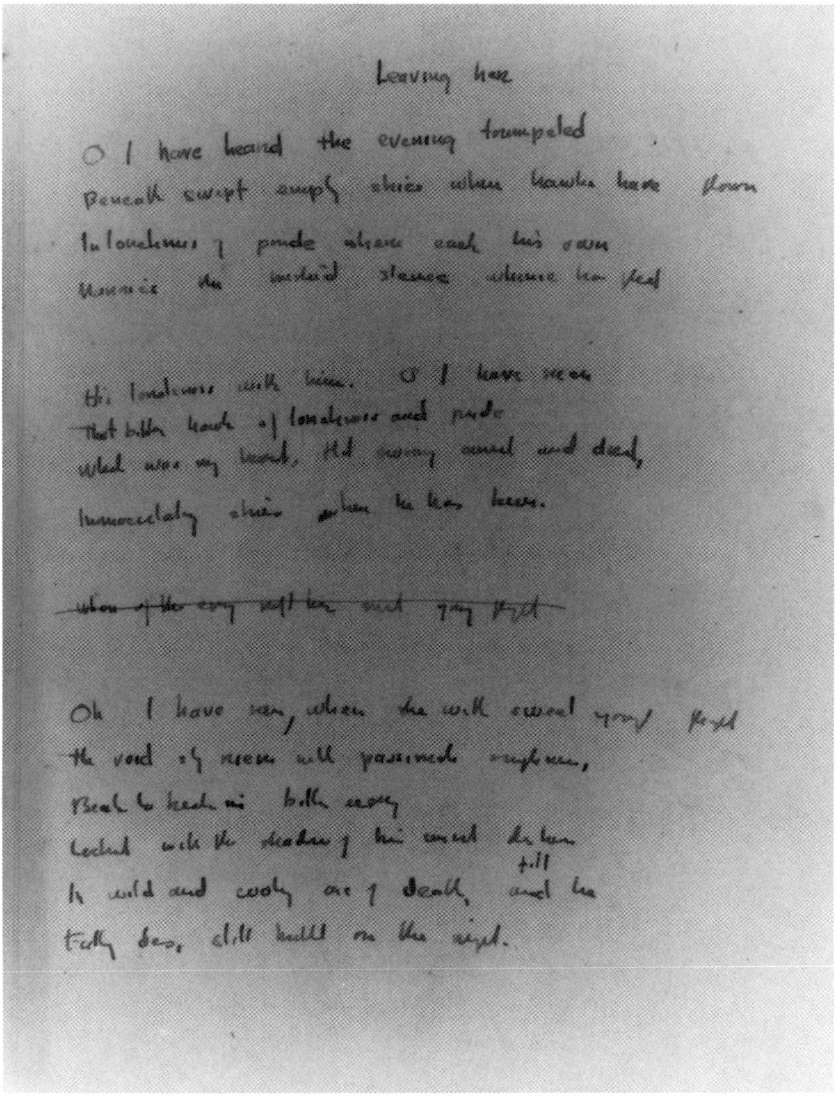

Figure 16.   Reproduction of Ink Holograph Draft
of McKeldin Library Version of "Leaving Her" (#60b)
*(Courtesy Jill Faulkner Summers and Special Collections,
University of Maryland College Park Libraries)*

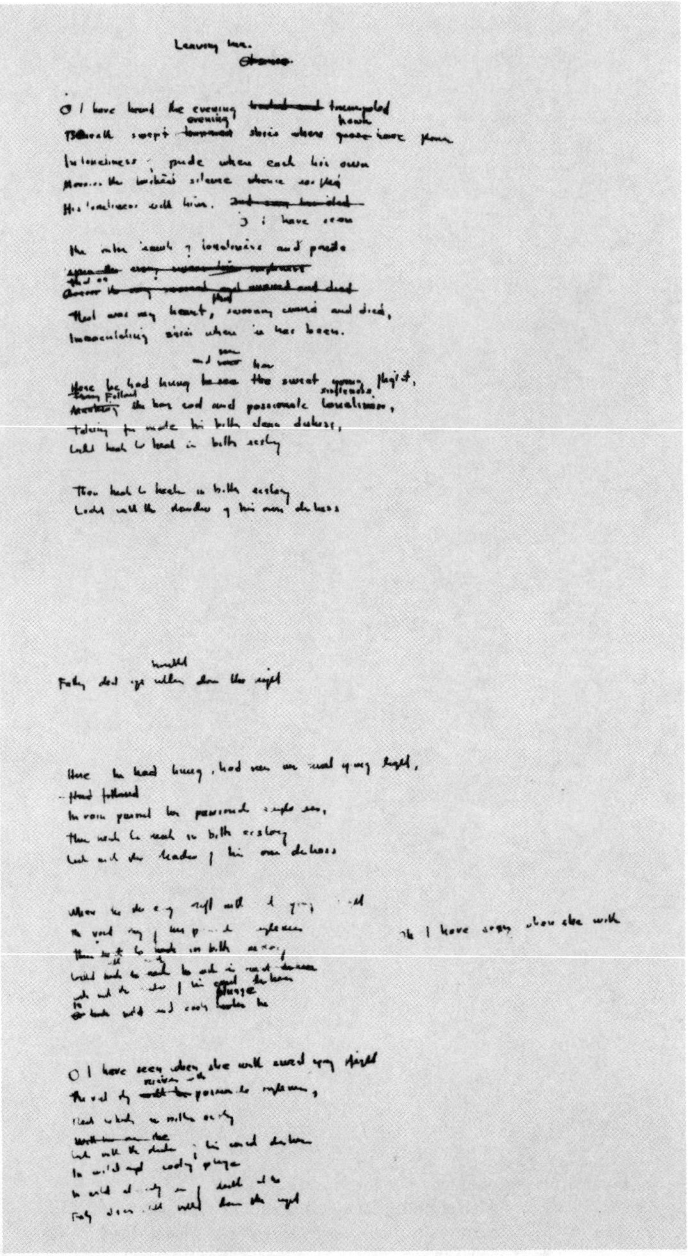

Figure 17. Reproduction of Ink Holograph Draft of
"Leaving Her"/"Obsession" (#60c)
(Courtesy Jill Faulkner Summers and Robert A. Wilson)

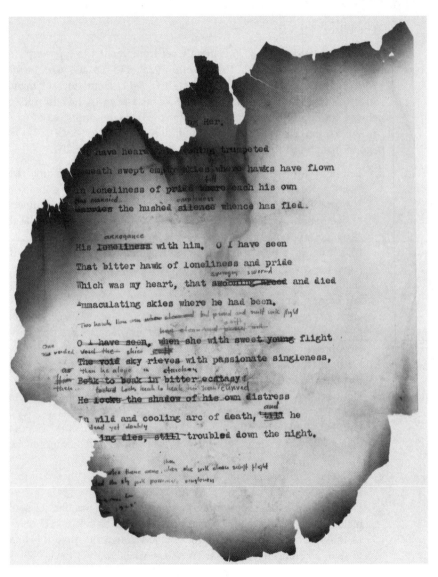

Figure 18.   Revised Typescript of "Leaving Her" (#60d)
(Courtesy Jill Faulkner Summers and the Harry Ransom
Humanities Research Center, The University of Texas, Austin)

1925," is the only known extant manuscript of the poem (see #163); LNT.

63. "The Lilacs" [*PV:36]

DD 7 (June 1925): 185–87 (apparently set from version in typescript (q) below. See *Wisdom:* 149). *Braithwaite 1925:* 115–18 and *Braithwaite 1959:* 275–78. *Salmagundi:* 47–51. *AGB* I: 7–11. Both sides of manuscript (n) reproduced in *Origins:* 62–63. First page of manuscript (o) below reproduced in *Selections:* 30 (figure 13). Manuscripts (k) through (n) and (o) through (p) transcribed and discussed in Brodsky 1983. One page of manuscript (o) reproduced in *Stylization:* 28 (figure 20).

a. Untitled, 1 p. typescript: 22 lines; canceled title and dedication read "The Lilacs / To A—— and H——, R.A.F., 1918"; note in Faulkner's hand reads, "Pub. Double Dealer 1924"; Roman numeral "I" at bottom of page; this is the first 22 lines of the poem; MsU (Rowan Oak, box 2, folder 43).

b. "The Lilacs," 1 p. typescript: burned fragment; this is a separate title page for a draft of the poem or for another copy of *The Lilacs* sequence with the title followed by "To A—— and H——, Royal Air Force. / August, 1918."; TxU.

c. Untitled, 1 p. typescript: burned fragment, 25 lines visible, 19 complete; first line "We sit drinking tea"; title and dedication typed above first line but erased; TxU.

d. Untitled, 1 p. typescript: burned fragment, 21 lines visible, 8 complete; first visible phrase "here, watching the young moon"; TxU.

e. Untitled, 1 p. typescript: burned fragment, 23 lines visible, 13 complete; first visible phrase "at its brink"; TxU.

f. Untitled, 1 p. typescript: burned fragment, 24 lines visible, 19 complete; first visible line "Stalking her through the shimmering reaches of the sky"; TxU.

g. Untitled, 1 p. carbon typescript: burned fragment, 23 lines visible, 9 complete; first visible phrase "you to talk"; TxU.

h. Untitled, 1 p. typescript: burned fragment, 25 lines visible, 22 complete; first line "Its well enough for one like you to talk"; TxU.

i. Untitled, 1 p. carbon typescript: burned fragment, final 11 lines visible, all complete; first line "We sit in silent amity"; TxU.

j. Untitled, 1 p. carbon typescript: burned fragment, 9 lines visible, 4 complete; first visible phrase "has followed the sun"; TxU.

k. "The Lilacs," 5 pp. carbon typescript: 99 lines; dedication at top reads "To A . . . and H . . . , Royal Air Force / August 1925"; at end is typed "William Faulkner 1925"; ViU (Accession #9817-b).

l. Untitled, 1 p. ink holograph manuscript fragment on legal-size paper: 38 lines; first line "And found her at the border of a wood"; additional 41 lines in pencil on other side; ViU (Accession #9817-b).

m. "The Lilacs," 2 pp. ink manuscript on legal-size paper: 62 lines; 57 penciled lines on other sides of both pages; ViU (Accession #9817-b).

n. Untitled, 1 p. manuscript: torn fragment, 26 lines visible, 24 complete, 5 canceled; first visible line "It was a morning in late May"; on the other side is an 11-line holograph fragment of the same poem beginning "One should not die like this"; ViU (Accession #9817-b).

o. Untitled, 5 pp. manuscript in 3 leaves; apparently early drafts, with deletions and revisions of material from "The Lilacs"; *H/B 1982:* 22.

p. "The Lilacs," 10 pp. manuscript: burned fragments, parts of 99 lines visible; this is *The Lilacs* I; *H/B 1982:* 26, pp. 5–14.

q. "The Lilacs," 3 pp. typescript: 68 lines; dedication reads: "To A. and H., Royal Air Force, August 1925"; LNT.

64. "Love Song" [*UV:28]

VIS: 55–64. Fragment from manuscript (a) below reproduced in *VIS:* Appendix B (p. xlvi). Quoted in *Origins:* 168–71 (figure 12) with relevant lines from Eliot's *Prufrock and Other Observations.*

a. "Love Song," 9 pp. photocopy of carbon typescript: 116 lines; bottoms of pages numbered consecutively from "55" to "64"; this is *Vision in Spring* IX; ViU (Accession #9817-I).
Note: On the obverse of the purple ribbon typescript listed below as [Texas] (#169) are penciled holograph fragments, five of which contain lines, phrases or passages that correspond with "Love Song." These fragments are listed as (b) through (f) below.

b. Untitled, 1 p. penciled manuscript: burned fragment, 15 lines visible, 10 complete; first visible phrase "that night has come"; TxU.

c. Untitled, 1 p. penciled manuscript: burned fragment, 17 lines visible, 12 complete; first visible phrase "alone. I will walk alone"; TxU.

d. Untitled, 1 p. penciled manuscipt: burned fragment, parts of 16 lines visible; first visible phrase "[tu?]rning endless pages"; first 8 lines correspond with "Love Song" and are followed by "II" and 8 lines which do not correspond with any poem in *VIS;* TxU.

e. Untitled, 1 p. penciled manuscript: burned fragment, 16 lines, none complete; first visible phrase "[team?]ing brain"; TxU.

f. Untitled, 1 p. penciled manuscript: burned fragment, 15 lines visible, 10 complete; first visible phrase "Does not each fold"; lines correspond with lines 79 through 82 and 100 through 109 of *VIS* [IX], pp. 61 and 63; TxU.

65. "La Lune ne Grade Aucune Rancune" [*PV:37]

    AGB XXXII: 55. Typescript (a) reproduced in *Meriwether:* figure 4.

    a. "La Lune ne Grade Aucune Rancune," 1 p. purple ribbon typescript: 6 lines; first line "Look, Cynthia"; at bottom is typed an inscription for Sam Gilmore; ViU (Accession #6074).

66. "Man Comes, Man Goes" [*PV:38]

    Published as "Man Comes, Man Goes" in *NR* 74 (3 May 1933): 338. *AGB* VI: 24.

    a. Untitled, 1 p. purple ribbon typescript: 8 lines; first line "Man comes, man goes; and leaves behind"; "(1)" at bottom of page partially erased; "2" and "1" penciled and circled at bottom; this is included in [*Virginia 1*] (#170); ViU (Accession #6074).
    b. Untitled, 1 p. carbon typescript: burned fragment, parts of 8 lines visible; first visible phrase "last in dust"; TxU.
    c. Untitled, 1 p. typescript: burned fragment, 8 lines visible, first 6 complete; TxU.
    d. Untitled, 1 p. typescript: burned fragment, parts of 4 lines visible; first visible phrase "[wishi?]ng's utmost rim"; "W[ill?]iam Faulkner" typed below poem; TxU.
    e. Untitled, 1 p. carbon typescript: burned fragment, 8 lines visible, 4 complete; first visible phrase "and leaves behind"; TxU.

67. "March" [*PV:61]

    AGB XLII: 65. *HC/MP:* 113 and 158. Typescript (g) reproduced in *MP 1979:* 29. Manuscript (f) reproduced in *HC 1981:* n.p. Collins 1981 quotes the *AGB* version of this poem and compares it to the *HC* version: 43.

    a. Untitled, 1 p. typescript: sonnet; first line "Beneath the apple tree Eve's tortured shape"; MsU (Rowan Oak, box 2, folder 40).
    b. "March," 1 p. typescript: 14 lines not in sonnet form; at bottom left in ink holograph "15 December 24"; NN-B.
    c. "Sonnet," 1 p. typescript: burned fragment, 15 lines visible, 9 complete; "[Fau?]lkner" typed in upper left corner; TxU.
    d. Untitled, 1 p. black ribbon typescript: burned fragment, 16 lines visible, 9 complete; first visible phrase "Eve's tortured shape"; ink holograph "1924" below poem; TxU.

   e. Untitled, 1 p. black ribbon typescript: burned fragment, parts of 13 lines visible; first visible phrase "the apple tree Eve's tortured shape"; TxU.

   f. Untitled, 1 p. manuscript: sonnet; dated "PASCAGOULA-JUNE-1925"; this is *Helen: A Courtship* II; LNT.

   g. "March," 1 p. carbon typescript: sonnet; this is one of Brodsky's unsequenced *Mississippi Poems; H/B 1982:* 451.

68. *The Marionettes* [*UV:19 and 43]

For published versions, see short title listing, *TM*. See also ["Those cries, like scatt[ered silve?]r sails"], #108, for a published poem that combines lines from *TM* and lines from *TMF*.

   a. *The Marionettes / A Play in One Act,* holograph manuscript: 42 leaves, 56 numbered pages, 10 illustrations by author; bound by Faulkner, 1920; rebound by Ben Wasson in the 1930s; on first blank leaf is Ben Wasson's signature. This version, the earliest, is substantially different from the other 3 known copies; ViU (Accession #6271-AK).

   b. *Marionettes / A Play in One Act,* holograph manuscript: 42 leaves, 51 numbered pages, 10 illustrations by author; bound by Faulkner; MsU.

   c. *Marionettes / A Play in One Act,* holograph manuscript: 42 leaves, 51 numbered pages, 10 illustrations by author; bound by Faulkner; TxU.

   d. *Marionettes / A Play in One Act,* holograph manuscript: 42 leaves, 51 numbered pages, 10 illustrations by author; dedication written in upper case reads "To 'Cho-cho' / a tiny flower of the flame, the /eternal gesture chrystallized; / this, a shadowy fumbling in / windy darkness, is most re- / spectfully tendered. / First edition 1920"; hand-bound by author; TxU.

69. "Marriage" [*PV:40]

VIS: 67–75. *AGB* II: 12–15.

   a. Untitled, 9 pp. photocopy of carbon typescript: 102 lines; first line "Laxly reclining, he watches the firelight going"; bottoms of pages are consecutively numbered from "67" to "75"; this is *Vision in Spring* XI; ViU (Accession #9817-I).

   b. "Marriage," 4 pp. typescript: 83 lines; 1 holograph correction; at top of first page is ink holograph "8"; at bottoms of the four pages, in order, the numbers "9," "10," "11," and "12," each in parentheses, erased but legible; "William Faulkner" typed and canceled at bottom left on all 4 pages; this is included in [*Virginia 1*] (#170); ViU (Accession #6074).

c.   "Marriage," 4 pp. typescript: 78 lines; Roman numerals divide poem into 5 parts; "William Faulkner / Oxford, Mississippi" typed at top left of first page; page numbers typed at bottom of each page; MsU (Rowan Oak, box 2, folders 39 and 43).

d.   Untitled, 3 pp. black ribbon typescript: burned fragment, 38 lines visible, 32 complete; first visible phrase "[lan?]guid hands, palm up"; type and similarities in paper indicate that these leaves constitute a single typescript; TxU.

e.   Untitled, 1 p. black ribbon typescript: burned fragment, 13 lines visible, 10 complete, first visible phrase "Could she but drift"; TxU.

70.   "Mississippi Hills: My Epitaph" [*PV:41]

Published as "My Epitaph" in *Con* 1 (1 February 1932): 2 and *Wells:* 123. *HC/MP:* 156. Significantly different versions appear as *AGB* XLIV: 67; as "If There be Grief" in *James:* 33 and as *This Earth: A Poem by William Faulkner* in a limited edition printing (New York: Equinox, 1932) with illustrations by Albert Heckman (authorized facsimile reprinted on demand by University Microfilms International, Ann Arbor, Michigan, 1979). Typescript (d) reproduced in *Massey:* 76 (plate 5). Typescript (b) reproduced in both *Selections:* 42 (figure 18) and *MP 1979:* 27. Gresset 1982 prints French translations of both the 1924 version and the *AGB* version along with a discussion of the poem: 19–20.

a.   "My Epitaph," 1 p. black ribbon typescript: 2 quatrains; identical to *Con* version; ViU (Accession #6074).

b.   "VII. / Mississippi Hills: My Epitaph," 1 p. carbon typescript: 4 quatrains; "Mississippi Hills" added to title in holograph; typescript and holograph signatures; this is Brodsky's *Mississippi Poems* VII; *H/B 1982:* 45g.

c.   "VII / Mississippi Hills—My Epitaph," 1 p. ribbon typescript: 4 quatrains; "Mississippi Hills—" added to title in ink holograph; Roman numeral appears to have been corrected from "VI" to "VII" in ink; "William Faulkner" typed at end of page; end of final word blurred; this is Wynn *Mississippi Poems* VII; MsU (Wynn, folder 7, #40).

d.   "Mississippi Hills: My Epitaph," 1 p. black ribbon typescript: 4 quatrains; at bottom left is typed "Oxford, Mississippi / October 17, 1924" and at bottom right "William Faulkner"; ViU (Accession #6271).

e. Untitled, 1 p. typescript: burned fragment, 13 lines visible, 10 complete; first visible phrase "golden grief for grieving's sake"; 1 ink holograph correction; dateline at bottom "William Faulkner / Oxford, Miss. 16 October 1924"; TxU.

f. "[My Epit?]aph," 1 p. black ribbon typescript: burned fragment, 16 lines visible, 11 complete; TxU.

g. "My Epitaph," 1 p. carbon typescript: burned fragment, 16 lines visible in quatrains, 11 complete; this is the carbon of (f) above— together they give a complete draft of the poem; TxU.

71. ["Moon of death, moon of bright despair"] [*UF:35]

HC/MP: 150. Typescript (a) reproduced in *MP 1979:* 15.

a. Untitled, 1 p. carbon typescript: 4 quatrains; signed in holograph and typescript; this is Brodsky's *Mississippi Poems* II; *H/B 1982:* 45b.

b. Untitled, 1 p. ribbon typescript: 4 quatrains; "William Faulkner" typed at bottom; this is Wynn *Mississippi Poems* II; MsU (Wynn, folder 7, #34).

c. Untitled, 1 p. carbon typescript: burned fragment, 4 quatrains visible, all but last 6 lines complete; TxU.

72. ["My health? My health's a fevered loud distress"]

HC/MP: 117. Manuscript reproduced in *HC 1981:* n.p. This is *Helen: A Courtship* VI, dated "PASCAGOULA-JUNE-1925," the only known extant manuscript of the poem (see #163); LNT.

73. "Naiads' Song" [*PV:42]

Mis 4 February 1920: 3 and *EPP:* 55–6. No known extant manuscripts or typescripts.

74. "Night Piece" [*PV:44]

NR 74 (12 April 1933): 253. *AGB* VII: 25–26.

a. Untitled, 2 pp. carbon typescript on legal-size paper: 41 lines, 1 canceled; 1 penciled correction on first sheet; "XXVII" canceled above first line, "Trumpets of sun in silence fall"; penciled and circled "1" and "2" are written in margin of second page; on other side of second page, not in Faulkner's hand, is penciled note, "End of section"; this is included in [*Virginia 3*] (#172); ViU (Accession #6074).

b. Untitled, 1 p. carbon typescript: burned fragment, parts of 15 lines visible; first visible phrase "apple bough"; TxU.

c. Untitled, 1 p. carbon typescript: burned fragment, parts of 17 lines visible; first visible phrase "and munch their grain"; TxU.

d. Untitled, 1 p. black ribbon typescript: burned fragment, parts of 13 lines visible; first visible phrase "while far away"; TxU.

e. Untitled, 1 p. black ribbon typescript: burned fragment, parts of last 8 lines visible; first visible phrase "the murderer, bent of [kn?]ees"; TxU.

f. Untitled, 1 p. typescript: burned fragment, parts of 8 lines visible; first visible phrase "the murderer, bent of knees"; TxU.

g. Untitled, 1 p. carbon typescript: burned fragment, parts of last 7 lines visible; first visible phrase "murderer, bent"; TxU.

75. "November 11th" [*PV:46]

Titled "Gray the Day" when published in *NR* 74 (12 April 1933): 253. *AGB* XXX: 53. The last stanza, titled "Soldier," is epigraph for *Soldiers' Pay*. *HC/MP:* 159. Typescript (d) reproduced in *MP 1979:* 35. This is not the same poem as "The Husbandman," which was subtitled "November 11, 1941" and appears as *AGB* XXXI (#48).

a. "November 11," 1 p. pencil holograph manuscript on green Boni and Liveright memorandum sheet: 16 lines in quatrains; accompanying letter of authentication from John S. Clapp (assistant at Boni and Liveright when *Soldiers' Pay* was published), dated 15 April 1966, states that Faulkner transcribed the poem from memory shortly after the publication of *Soldiers' Pay;* MdU.

b. "Soldier," epigraph in *Soldiers' Pay* typescript: 4 lines; same as printed version except for two differences in accidentals; ViU.

c. "November 11," 1 p. typescript; 16 lines in quatrains; dated in holograph "11 November 24"; NN-B.

d. "November 11th," 1 p. carbon typescript: 4 quatrains; typed at bottom of page "Oxford, Mississippi. / November 11, 1924" and "William Faulkner"; holograph signature; this is unnumbered poem in Brodsky's *Mississippi Poems; H/B 1982:* 45j.

e. "November 11th," 1 p. ribbon typescript: burned edges but all lines complete, 4 quatrains; 7 holograph corrections; 9 differences in accidentals and ink holograph corrections indicate this was an earlier version of (d) above; typed dedication under title reads "In Memory of B——, Royal Air Force"; this is unsequenced poem in Wynn *Mississippi Poems;* MsU (Wynn, folder 5, #30).

f. "November 11," 1 p. black ribbon typescript: burned fragment, parts of 12 lines visible; TxU.

g. "November 11," 1 p. typescript: burned fragment, 15 lines visible, 9 complete; TxU.

76. "Ode to the Louver"

Carbon typescript (c) transcribed in Meriwether 1974. Typescript (a) reproduced in *H/B 1982:* 42–43 (figures 16–17).

a. "Ode to the Louver," 2 pp. typescript: 6 seven-line stanzas with "Orthurs notes" typed at bottom; *H/B 1982:* 54.

b. "Ode to the Louver," 2 pp. black ribbon typescript: 42 lines plus footnotes; TxU (catalogued under "Faulkner, W— Letters A–Z").

c. "Ode to the Louver," 2 pp. carbon typescript of (b) above with holograph corrections; TxU.

77. "Old Satyr" [*PV:47]

AGB XLI: 64. *HC/MP:* 115. Manuscript (d) reproduced in *HC 1981:* n.p.

a. Untitled, 1 p. typescript: sonnet; first line "Her unripe shallow breast is green among"; MsU (Rowan Oak, box 2, folder 40).

b. "Old Satyr," 1 p. black ribbon typescript: burned fragment, 14 lines visible, 13 complete; dated in Faulkner's hand "December, 1924"; TxU.

c. "[Ol?]d Satyr," 1 p. typescript: burned fragment, parts of 14 lines visible; TxU.

d. Untitled, 1 p. manuscript: sonnet; dated "PASCAGOULA-JUNE-1925"; this is *Helen: A Courtship* IV; LNT.

78. "On Seeing the Winged Victory for the First Time" [*PV:48]

AGB XVII: 39. Several lines quoted by Januarius Jones in *Soldiers' Pay:* 227. Quoted in Yonce 1970. *The Lilacs* version (i) quoted and compared to Pound's "O Atthis" in *Origins:* 241.

a. "On Seeing the Winged Victory for the First Time," 1 p. black ribbon typescript: 9 lines; penciled Arabic numerals "1" and "1" circled at bottom of poem; ViU (Accession #6074).

b. Untitled, 1 p. black ribbon typescript: burned fragment, 8 lines visible, 5 complete; first visible phrase "an aeon [i pa?]use plunging"; TxU.

MEMORANDUM

JULIAN MESSNER

To   November 11.

Gray the day and all the year is cold,
Across the empty land the swallows' cry
Marks the south-flown spring: naught is bowled
Save winter, in the sky.

O sorry earth, when this bleak bitter sleep
Stars and leaves and time once mine is gone
In empty path and lane grass will creep
With none to tread it clean.

April and May and June, and all the dearth
Of heart to green it for, to hurt and wake,
What good is budding, gray November earth?
No need to break your sleep for greening's sake.

The hushed plaint of wind in stricken trees
Shivers the grass in path and lane
And grief and time are tideless goldless seas —
Hush, hush! he's home again

Figure 19.   Penciled Holograph Manuscript of "November 11" (#75a)
(*Courtesy Jill Faulkner Summers and Special Collections, University of Maryland College Park Libraries*)

JOHN S. CLAPP

BOX 159

CHRISTIANSTED, ST. CROIX

U. S. VIRGIN ISLANDS
—
PHONE: C-79W

One afternoon, shortly after SOLDIER'S PAY was published,* I was sitting in Julian Messner's office. Both
Julian and Horace were out. The phone rang, and William Faulkner was announced.

He came in a moment later,- a young man with a rather
heavy square-cut brown beard that made his smiling,
soft brown eyes even softer.

He seemed quite shy until we got onto the subject of
his book, and I told him with complete sincerity how
much I had enjoyed reading it. I had read it in gal-
lies, and had noted at the time a four-line dedication in verse, which I had also liked. When I asked
him its source he smiled, reached over onto Julian's
desk for a memo pad, and wrote out the four verses of
NOVEMBER 11, which I suddenly realised he had written
himself. The last verse was the one used as a dedication.

At that time I was Julian Messner's assistant at Boni
& Liveright.

April 15, 1966

* 1926

Figure 20.   Letter from John S. Clapp Explaining When Faulkner
Transcribed "November 11"
Clapp was Julian Messner's assistant at Boni and Liveright in 1926.
(Courtesy Special Collections, University of Maryland College Park Libraries)

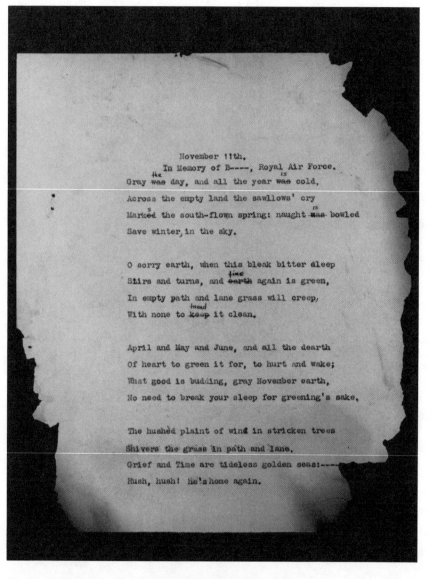

Figure 21.   "November 11th" with Dedication (#75e)
*(Courtesy Jill Faulkner Summers and the John Davis Williams
Library, University of Mississippi)*

c. "[On Seeing the Winged Victory for?] the First Time," 1 p. black ribbon typescript: burned fragment, parts of 6 lines and title visible; TxU.

d. Untitled, 1 p. black ribbon typescript: burned fragment, parts of 8 lines visible; first visible word "plunging"; TxU.

e. Untitled, 1 p. carbon typescript: burned fragment, parts of 8 lines visible; first visible phrase "I pause"; TxU.

f. Untitled, 1 p. black ribbon typescript: burned fragment, parts of 8 lines visible; first visible word "aeon"; TxU.

g. "[On Seeing the Winged Victor?]y for the First Time," 1 p. carbon typescript: burned fragment, parts of 7 lines and title visible; TxU.

h. Untitled, 1 p. typescript: 7 lines, first line "O Atthis"; NN-B.

i. "O Atthis," 1 p. manuscript: burned fragment, 8 lines visible, 6 complete; this is *The Lilacs* V; *H/B 1982:* 26, p. 19.

79. "An Orchid"

Photocopy of manuscript reproduced in *Stylization:* 87 (figures 83–85).

a. "An Orchid," 1 p. photocopy of holograph manuscript: 5 lines; this is one of the [*Estelle Poems*] (#161); location of original unknown, photocopy ViU (Accession #9817-I).

80. "Orpheus" [*PV:49]

VIS: 76–82. *AGB* XX: 42 comprises the first 13 lines and lines 23 through 36 of the *VIS* version. *AGB* version published with the title "Here He Stands" in *James:* 33. Typescript (b) reproduced in *VIS:* Appendix B (p. xliv–xlv).

a. "Orpheus," 7 pp. photocopy of carbon typescript: 79 lines; bottoms of pages numbered consecutively from "76" to "82"; this is *Vision in Spring* XII; ViU (Accession #9817-I).

b. "Orpheus," 2 pp. typescript: burned fragments, 43 lines visible, 40 complete; CtY.

81. "Pastoral"

Transcribed in *Man Collecting:* 127.

a. "Pastoral," 1 p. purple ribbon typescript: 4 quatrains; ViU (Accession #6271-AK).

82. "Philosophy" [*PV:50]

    AGB V: 22–23; *VIS:* 83–85.

    a. "Philosophy," 3 pp. photocopy of carbon typescript: 30 lines; bottoms of pages numbered consecutively "83," "84," and "85"; this is *Vision in Spring* XIII; ViU (Accession #9817-I).
    b. "Philosophy," 2 pp. purple ribbon typescript: 6 five-line strophes, 1 penciled correction apparently not in Faulkner's hand; typed, canceled "21" and "22" at bottoms of pages; "William Faulkner" typed and canceled at bottoms of pages; although unnumbered, this is included in [*Virginia 1*] (#170); ViU (Accession #6074).
    c. Untitled, 1 p. black ribbon typescript: burned fragment, 15 lines visible, 12 complete; first visible phrase "No footfall trembles in the smoky"; 1 ink holograph correction; TxU.
    d. Untitled, 1 p. typescript: burned fragment, parts of 2 lines visible; only visible phrase "sharp and cold"; TxU.
    e. Untitled, 1 p. black ribbon typescript: burned fragment, part of 1 line visible; only visible words "and cold"; TxU.
    f. Untitled, 1 p. black ribbon typescript: burned fragment, parts of last 5 lines visible; first visible phrase "sadness, nor does any l[ife?]"; "William Faulkner" typed at bottom; TxU.
    g. Untitled, 1 p. black ribbon typescript: burned fragment, 14 lines visible, 1 complete; first visible phrase "the dappled shade"; TxU.
    h. Untitled, 1 p. carbon typescript: burned fragment, 13 lines visible, 1 complete; first visible phrase "brush / [?] the dappled shade"; ink holograph corrections, not in Faulkner's hand, in right margin; TxU.

83. "Pierrot, Sitting Beside the Body of Colombine, suddenly Sees Himself in a Mirror" [*UV:25]

    Transcribed in Meriwether 1982 and in *Origins:* 231–32, n. 8.

    a. "Pierrot, Sitting Beside the Body of Colombine, suddenly Sees Himself in a Mirror," 3 pp. purple ribbon typescript: 64 lines in 8 stanzas; at the bottom is typed "William Faulkner"; in pencil at bottom of last page is note (not in Faulkner's hand): "Written while visiting in the house / of Mr & Mrs Ben F. Wasson / in 1921"; this is included in Brodsky's [*Aunt Bama Poems*], but not sequenced by Faulkner; *H/B 1982:* 18.1.

84. "The Poet Goes Blind" [*UV:26]

    HC/MP: 155. Typescript (a) reproduced in *H/B 1982:* 39 (figure 15) and in *MP 1979:* 25.

    a. "VI. / The Poet Goes Blind," 1 p. typescript: 4 five-line stanzas; holograph signature at bottom; also typed at bottom "William Faulkner / Oxford, Mississippi, / 29 Oct. 1924"; this is Brodsky's *Mississippi Poems* VI; *H/B 1982:* 45f.
    b. "The Poet Goes Blind," 1 p. typescript: burned but complete with 4 five-line stanzas; "VI" in pen over title; 1 ink holograph correction in last line; signed in black ink holograph, "William Faulkner / Oxford / 29 October 1924"; this is Wynn *Mississippi Poems* VI; MsU (Wynn, folder 7, #39).
    c. "The Poet Goes Blind," 1 p. carbon typescript: burned fragment, 4 five-line stanzas visible, 15 lines complete; identical to published version except for changes in accidentals; TxU.

85. "A Poplar" [*PV:51]

    Mis 17 March 1920: 7 and *EPP:* 60. No known extant manuscripts or typescripts.

86. "Portrait" [*PV:52]

    VIS: 33–35. The version in *DD* 3 (June 1922): 337, *EPP:* 99–100, and *Salmagundi:* 45–46 has 14 variants from the *VIS* version. Morton prints the *DD* version along with the Hemingway poem, "Ultimately," which appeared on the same page: 255.

    a. "Portrait," 3 pp. photocopy of carbon typescript: 24 lines; bottoms of pages numbered consecutively "33," "34," and "35"; this is *Vision in Spring* V; ViU (Accession #9817-I).
    b. "Portrait," 1 p. black ribbon typescript: burned fragment, 19 lines visible, 13 complete; black ink holograph "3." above title; TxU.

87. "Pregnacy" [*sic*] [*PV:53]

    AGB XXIX: 52. *HC/MP:* 161. Manuscript (c) reproduced in *H/B 1982:* 31 (figure 10). Typescript (d) reproduced in *H/B 1982:* 34 (figure 12) and in *MP 1979:* 33. *Note: Poem's title is misspelled on all extant versions.*

    a. "Pregnacy," 1 p. black ribbon typescript: burned fragment, parts of 12 lines visible; TxU.

    b. Untitled, 1 p. typescript: burned fragment, 16 lines visible, 8 complete; first visible phrase "music's hidden fall"; TxU.

    c. "Pregnacy," 1 p. brown ink and penciled holograph manuscript written on other side of letterhead stationery of Dr. Willis C. Campbell, Memphis, Tennessee: 4 quatrains; 4 corrections; Brodsky states that Faulkner wrote the poem for Mrs. Homer K. Jones while visiting her home in Memphis during the week of 23 November 1924; *H/B 1982:* 38.

    d. "Pregnacy," 1 p. carbon typescript: 4 quatrains; 2 holograph corrections; typed beneath the poem are "Oxford, Mississippi / November 10, 1924." and "William Faulkner"; *H/B 1982:* 40.

    e. "Pregnacy," 1 p. carbon typescript; typed and holograph signature at bottom; also typed at bottom is "Oxford, Mississippi / November 10, 1924"; this is one of Brodsky's unsequenced *Mississippi Poems; H/B 1982:* 45i.

88. "Proposal" [*PV:32]

AGB XLIII: 66. *HC/MP:* 116. Manuscript (e) reproduced in *HC 1981:* n.p.

    a. Untitled, 1 p. typescript: sonnet; 2 corrections; MsU (Rowan Oak, box 2, folder 39).

    b. "In Spring a Young Man's Fancy——," 1 p. black ribbon typescript: burned fragment, sonnet with 13 lines visible, 9 complete; TxU.

    c. Untitled, 1 p. black ribbon typescript: burned fragment, 14 lines visible, 11 complete; first visible line "Let's see, I'll say: Between two brief balloons"; TxU.

    d. "[In Spr?]ing a Young Man's Fancy——," 1 p. typescript: burned fragment, 14 lines visible, 10 complete; 9 holograph revisions; "off Minorca / 1 Aug 1925" typed below poem; TxU.

    e. "Proposal," 1 p. holograph manuscript: sonnet; at bottom is written "PASCAGOULA-JUNE-1925"; this is *Helen: A Courtship* V; LNT.

89. "Puck and Death" [*PV:54]

AGB XVI: 37–38. *James:* 31 (titled "Mirror of Youth").

    a. Puck and Death," 1 p. purple ribbon typescript on legal-size paper: 6 quatrains; ink holograph quotation marks at beginning and end of each strophe; "William Faulkner" (canceled) and "(7)" (erased) at bottom of page; this is included in [*Virginia 1*] (#170); text differs slightly from *AGB* XVI; ViU (Accession #6074).

b. Untitled, 1 p. typescript: burned fragment, 2 full lines and 1 partial line; first line "Behold me in my feathered cap and doublet"; MsU (Rowan Oak, box 2, folder 39).

c. "Puck and Death," 1 p. typescript: burned fragment, first 16 lines complete; 1 ink holograph correction; TxU.

d. Untitled, 1 p. carbon typescript: burned fragment, parts of 15 lines visible; first visible phrase "and doublet"; TxU.

e. Untitled, 1 p. black ribbon typescript: burned fragment, parts of 15 lines visible; first visible line (fourth line) "belief you, too, are but a mortal"; TxU.

f. Untitled, 1 p. black ribbon typescript: burned fragment, 8 lines visible and complete; first visible line "Ho . . . one grows weary, posturing and grinning"; "William Faulkner" typed at bottom left; TxU.

90. "The Race's Splendor" [*PV:13]

Titled "The Race's Splendor" in *NR* 74 (12 April 1933): 253. *AGB* XXXVII: 60.

a. "Cleopatra," 1 p. black ribbon typescript on legal-size paper: sonnet; "8" in ink above title; dated in Faulkner's hand "9 December 1924"; a version of *AGB* XXXVII with "Lilith" substituted for "Cleopatra" in line 9; ViU (Accession #6074).

91. ["Rain, rain . . . a field of silver grain"]

VIS: 47–54.

a. Untitled, 8 pp. photocopy of carbon typescript: 92 lines; lines 30–31 have overstrike and penciled corrections; bottoms of pages numbered consecutively "47" through "54"; this is *Vision in Spring* VIII and appears to be a unique copy of the poem; ViU (Accession #9817-I).

92. ["The Raven bleak and Philomel"] [*PV:55]

AGB XXVII: 49–50. Stanzas 4, 1, and 2 of the *AGB* poem appeared in *Mosquitoes:* 246–47.

a. Untitled, *Mosquitoes* typescript, ff. 329–30: 3 four-line stanzas; first line "On rose and peach their droppings bled"; this is the same as the printed version except for several minor differences in accidentals; ViU.

b. Untitled, 1 p. typescript: 24 lines in quatrains; 1 ink holograph correction; at bottom left in ink holograph is "1 March 25"; NN-B.

c. Untitled, 1 p. typescript: 24 lines in quatrains; a later draft of type-script (b) above; NN-B.

d. Untitled, 1 p. black ribbon typescript: burned fragment, 8 lines visible, 5 complete; first visible phrase "on pain's red rose"; TxU.

e. Untitled, 2 pp. carbon typescript: 7 quatrains visible and complete; at bottom left is typed "Oxford, Mississippi, / February 26, 1925."; at bottom right is typed "William Faulkner."; TxU.

f. Untitled, 1 p. black ribbon typescript: burned fragment, 18 lines visible, 8 complete; first visible phrase "and Philom[el?]"; TxU.

g. Untitled, 1 p. black ribbon typescript: burned fragment, 20 lines visible, 13 complete; first visible phrase "[R?]aven bleak and Philo-mel"; TxU.

h. Untitled, 1 p. black ribbon typescript: burned fragment, 8 lines visible, 4 complete; at bottom left is typed "Oxford, Mississippi, / February 26, 1925"; at bottom right is typed "William Faulkner."; TxU.

93. ["Red thy famble"]

8-line poem quoted in *Wilde:* 77. This version and another, similar, 4-line version quoted and compared to Richard Head's fourth canting song in Collins 1981: 61–63. Also quoted and discussed by Minter 1980: 162. No manuscripts or typescripts available.

94. "Roland" [*PV:56]

AGB XXI: 43.

a. "Roland," 1 p. purple ribbon typescript: burned fragment, 4 quatrains visible, 3 quatrains complete; penciled Arabic numeral "1" circled in lower left corner below poem; TxU.

b. Untitled, 1 p. purple ribbon typescript: burned fragment, 3 quatrains visible, 10 lines complete; first visible phrase "feel the sharp goads of your eyes"; TxU.

c. Untitled, 1 p. typescript: burned fragment, parts of 15 lines visible; first visible phrase "scroll and"; TxU.

d. Untitled, 1 p. carbon typescript: burned fragment, 16 lines visible, 6 complete; first visible phrase "scroll and"; TxU.

e. Untitled, 1 p. carbon typescript: burned fragment, parts of 13 lines visible; first visible word "sighs?"; TxU.

f. Untitled, 1 p. purple ribbon typescript: burned fragment, 8 lines visible, 4 complete; first visible phrase "valiant foemen"; "William Faulkner" typed below poem; TxU.

g. "Roland," 1 p. carbon typescript: burned fragment, 12 lines visible, 7 complete; TxU.

95. "Sapphics" [*PV:57]

Mis 26 November 1919: 3. *EPP:* 51–52. Quoted and compared to Algernon Swinburne's "Sapphics" in Richardson 1969: 63 and in *Origins:* 78–90.

a. Untitled, burned fragment: parts of 24 lines visible; first visible phrase "not on my eyelids"; this is *The Lilacs* XI; *H/B 1982:* 26, pp. 28–30.

96. ["Se tiarait coup de fusee aimez vous la Française"]

6-line poem quoted in *Wilde:* 74. No manuscripts or typescripts available.

97. ["Shall I recall this tree, when I am old"] [*PV:58]

HC/MP: 149. Typescript (a) reproduced in *Massey:* 77 (figure vi). Typescript (e) reproduced in *MP 1979:* 13.

a. Untitled, 1 p. black ribbon typescript: 4 quatrains; at bottom left is typed "Oxford, Mississippi. / October 18, 1924."; at bottom right "William Faulkner."; ViU (Accession #6074).

b. Untitled, 1 p. black ribbon typescript on legal-size parchment paper: 4 quatrains; above first line is typed Arabic numeral "1."; ViU (Accession #6074).

c. Untitled, 1 p. carbon typescript: burned, but all 4 quatrains are complete; Arabic numeral "1." at top; TxU.

d. Untitled, 1 p. typescript: 4 quatrains; the words "Mississippi Poems" are canceled but visible above the Roman numeral "I" that precedes poem; at bottom left is typed "William Faulkner"; this is the Wynn *Mississippi Poems* I; MsU (Wynn, folder 7, #33).

e. Untitled, 1 p. carbon typescript: 4 quatrains; at bottom typed and signed "William Faulkner"; this is Brodsky's *Mississippi Poems* I; *H/B 1982:* 45a.

98. ["She is like a tower of warm ivory"]

Transcribed in *Bonner:* 3.

a. Untitled, 1 p. holograph manuscript on lined paper: 9 lines; signed "William Faulkner"; illustrated with apparent self-caricature; paper folder for poem reads "Poem / inside" followed by first line; LNT.

99.   "She Lies Sleeping" [*PV:59]

   AGB XL: 63.

   a.   "She Lies Sleeping," 1 p. typescript: sonnet; MsU (Rowan Oak, box 2, folder 39).

100.   "The Ship of Night" [*PV:43]

   NR 74 (19 April 1933): 272. *AGB* XXXIV: 57. Published as "Mother and Child" in *James:* 34–35.

   a.   "Nativity," 1 p. black ribbon typescript on legal-size paper: sonnet; 1 penciled holograph correction; text differs slightly from *AGB* XXXIV; ViU (Accession #6074).

101.   ["Somewhere is spring with green and simple gold"] [*PV:60]

   HC/MP: 125. Manuscript (a) reproduced in *HC 1981:* n.p. The final sestet of this poem appears as *AGB* XXIII: 45 with major changes.

   a.   Untitled, 1 p. holograph manuscript: sonnet; this is *Helen: A Courtship* XIV, dated "PARIS-SEPTEMBER-1925," the only known extant version of the poem (see #163); LNT.

102.   "A Song"

   Quoted in *Blotner 1974:* 195. Photocopied manuscript (a) reproduced in *Origins:* 217 and *Stylization:* 87 (figures 83-5). Blotner also quotes 4 variant lines from a typescript that has not been located: 195.

   a.   "A Song," 1 p. photocopy of ink holograph manuscript: 8 lines; this is one of the [*Estelle Poems*] (#161); location of original unknown; photocopy, ViU (Accession #9817-I).

103.   "Spring" [*PV:62]

   Con 1 (1 February 1932): 2. *AGB* XXXVI: 59. Text of both *Contempo* and *AGB* versions are quoted in Garrett 1973: 49–50.

   a.   "Spring," 1 p. black ribbon typescript: sonnet; first line "Gusty trees windily lean on green"; "14" penciled above title; dated in Faulkner's hand "13 December, 1924"; ViU (Accession #6074).

104. "Streets" [*PV:63]

Mis 17 March 1920: 2 and *EPP:* 59. No known extant manuscripts or typescripts.

105. "Study" [*PV:64]

Mis 21 April 1920: 4 and *EPP:* 62–63. No known extant manuscripts or typescripts.

106. ["The sun lies long upon the hills"] [*PV:65]

AGB IX: 29.

 a. Untitled, 1 p. black ribbon typescript on legal-size paper: 4 quatrains; above first line is typed "4"; text differs slightly from *AGB* IX; this is included in [*Virginia 2*] (#171); ViU (Accession #6074).
 b. Untitled, 1 p. typescript: burned fragment, 13 lines visible, 8 complete; first visible line "The sun sank down, and with him went"; TxU.
 c. Untitled, purple ribbon typescript: 4 quatrains; this is [*Aunt Bama Poems*] I; *H/B 1982:* 18a; aperture cards ViU (Accession #6074, box 11, #20).
 d. Untitled, 1 p. typescript: burned fragment, 16 lines visible, all but last line complete; first line "The sun lay long upon the hills"; other substantive changes throughout; MsU (Wynn, folder 8, #41).

107. "A Symphony" [*UV:33 and *UF:41]

VIS: 40–46.

 a. Untitled, 7 pp. photocopy of carbon typescript: 115 lines; line 41 canceled but legible; first line "The dark ascends"; "A Symphony" penciled at top, but not in Faulkner's hand; bottoms of pages numbered consecutively "40" through "46"; illegible lines written at bottom of final page; this is *Vision in Spring* VII; ViU (Accession #9817-I).
 b. "Symphony," 4 pp. black ribbon typescript: burned fragment, 92 lines visible, 59 complete; black ink holograph "7." above title; TxU.
 c. Untitled, 4 pp. carbon typescript: burned fragment, 90 lines visible, 79 complete; line ends of first strophe "climbs / clarinet / regret /again / pain / horn"; "William Faulkner" typed in ribbon at bottom; paper and type indicate that these leaves constitute a single typescript; TxU.

108. ["Those cries, like scatt[ered silve?]r sails"]

Manuscripts (a) and (b) informally collated and transcribed, and link between *TMF* and *TM* discussed in Polk 1977: xxviii–xxix. Manuscript (c) transcribed and discussed in Sensibar 1979.

  a. Untitled, 2 pp. black ribbon typescript: burned fragment, 40 lines visible, 23 complete; first page, beginning "Those cries like scatt[ered silve?]r sails," includes 1 penciled revision, probably in Phil Stone's hand, which is incorporated into typescript (b), indicating that this is an earlier version; second page, beginning "You are a trembling pool," has 1 penciled holograph note, probably in Phil Stone's hand, "[Pr?]obably will omit song from here on"; versions of lines 1, 2, and 5 through 8 correspond to *TMF,* p. 33; lines 15 through 33 appear in *TM,* pp. 19–21; final lines (34 through 39) are variants of *TMF,* pp. 50–51; TxU.

  b. Untitled, 2 pp. black ribbon typescript: burned fragment, 40 lines visible, 21 complete; first visible phrase on first page "azure sea"; first visible phrase on second page "me that only you can quench"; TxU.

  c. Untitled, 44 holograph lines written at end of Faulkner's copy of Ralph Hodgson's *Poems;* first line "Your little feet have crossed my heart"; this is an earlier (?) version of lines 18 through 46 of (a) and (b) above; JFS, xerox at ViU (Accession #9817-I, listed as "3 pp. in pencil of William Faulkner's poetry on terminal end papers of Ralph Hodgson's *Poems*").

109. "To a Co-ed" [*PV:66]

OMY: 174 and *EPP:* 70.

  a. "To a Co-ed," 1 p. holograph manuscript: burned fragment, parts of 14 lines visible; this is *The Lilacs* III; *H/B 1982:* 26, p. 17.

110. ["to dust? Should we then, li[ke?]"]

Both sides of this leaf are reproduced in *Origins:* 110 and 112.

  a. Untitled, 1 p. purple ribbon typescript: burned fragment, 22 lines visible, 15 complete; the final lines are variants of the refrain in *VIS* IX, "Love Song," but the typescript is [*Texas*], leaf AA (#169); on the other side is a penciled holograph draft version of Faulkner's 1921 review of Conrad Aiken's *Turns and Movies* beginning "In the fog of generic puberty raised by contemp[orary?] ve[rsifiers?]"; TxU.

111. "To Helen, Swimming"

HC/MP: 111. Manuscript reproduced in *HC 1981:* n.p. This is the dedi-catory poem of *Helen: A Courtship,* dated "PASCAGOULA-JUNE-1925," the only known manuscript of the poem (see #163); LNT.

112. ["Turn again, Dick Whittington!"] [*UF:9]

Transcribed in *Selections:* 25.

   a. Untitled, 1 p. purple ribbon typescript: 5 quatrains; this is [*Aunt Bama Poems*] III; *H/B 1982:* 18c; aperture cards ViU (Accession #6074, box 11, #20).
   b. Untitled, last 4 quatrains of [*Housman*], leaf B: burned fragment, 4 quatrains complete except for last letter of one word; "VI." typed above poem; similar to published version except for slight substantive variants and missing final quatrain; this is [*Housman*] VI; MsU (Wynn, folder 10, #11).
   c. Untitled, 1 p. purple ribbon typescript: burned fragment, 12 lines visible, 11 complete; first visible line "As tomorrow I shall be"; "William Faulkner." typed at bottom; identical to last 3 stanzas of (a) above; TxU.

113. "Twilight" [*PV:68]

Con 1 (1 February 1932): 1. *AGB* X: 30. Also in *Wells:* 126.

   a. Untitled, 1 p. black ribbon typescript: 5 quatrains; "Twilight" in pencil, not in Faulkner's hand, has been erased; below title is typed "5"; first line "Beyond the hill the sun swam downward"; text identi-cal to *Con* version; this is included in [*Virginia 2*] (#171); ViU (Accession #6074).
   b. Untitled, 1 p. purple ribbon typescript: burned fragment, 11 lines visible, 8 complete; first visible line "Nymph and faun, in this dusk, might riot"; 1 ink holograph revision; TxU.
   c. Untitled, 1 p. black ribbon typescript: burned fragment, parts of 11 lines visible; first visible phrase "whipped him"; TxU.
   d. Untitled, 1 p. carbon typescript: burned fragment, parts of 12 lines visible; first visible phrase "whipped him"; appears to be a carbon of (c) above; TxU.
   e. Untitled, 1 p. carbon typescript: burned fragment, parts of 12 lines visible; first visible phrase "whipped him"; appears to be a carbon of (c) above; TxU.

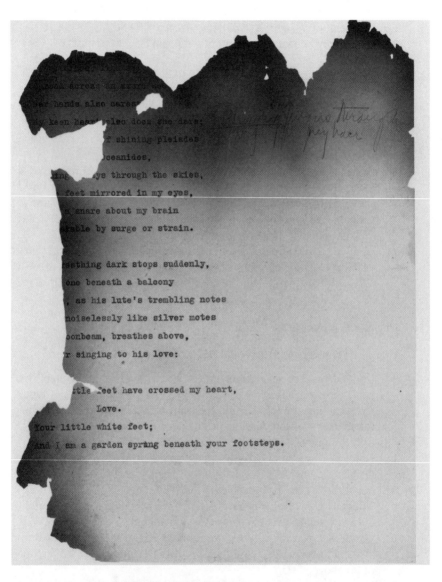

Figure 22. Typescript of First Leaf of ["Those cries like
scatt[ered silve?]r sails"] (#108a)
*(Courtesy Jill Faulkner Summers and the Harry Ransom
Humanities Research Center, The University of Texas, Austin)*

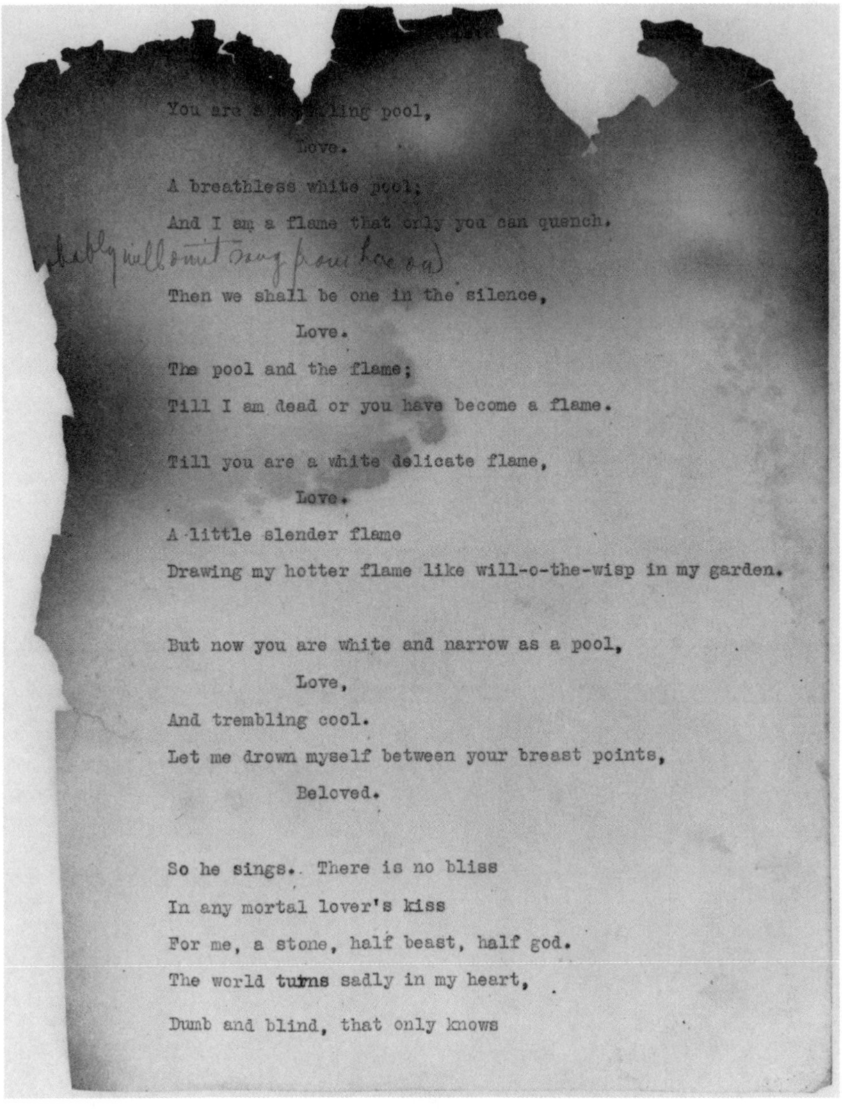

You are a [illegible]ling pool,
              Love.

A breathless white pool;
And I am a flame that only you can quench.
[handwritten: probably will omit song from here on)]
Then we shall be one in the silence,
              Love.
The pool and the flame;
Till I am dead or you have become a flame.

Till you are a white delicate flame,
              Love.
A little slender flame
Drawing my hotter flame like will-o-the-wisp in my garden.

But now you are white and narrow as a pool,
              Love,
And trembling cool.
Let me drown myself between your breast points,
              Beloved.

So he sings. There is no bliss
In any mortal lover's kiss
For me, a stone, half beast, half god.
The world turns sadly in my heart,
Dumb and blind, that only knows

Figure 23. Typescript of Second Leaf of ["Those cries like
scatt[ered silve?]r sails"] (#108a)
*(Courtesy Jill Faulkner Summers and the Harry Ransom
Humanities Research Center, The University of Texas, Austin)*

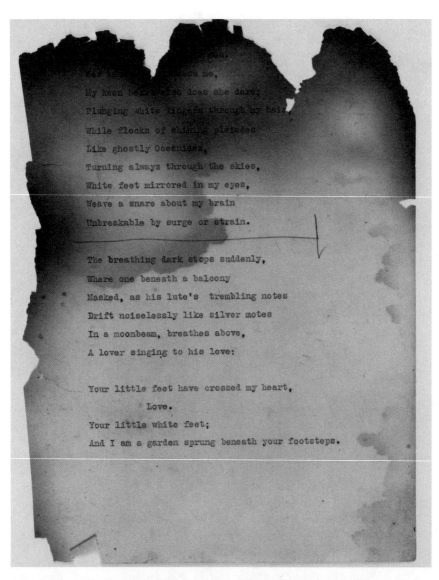

Figure 24.   Typescript of First Leaf of Poem Fragment ["azure sea"] (#108b)
*(Courtesy Jill Faulkner Summers and the Harry Ransom
Humanities Research Center, The University of Texas, Austin)*

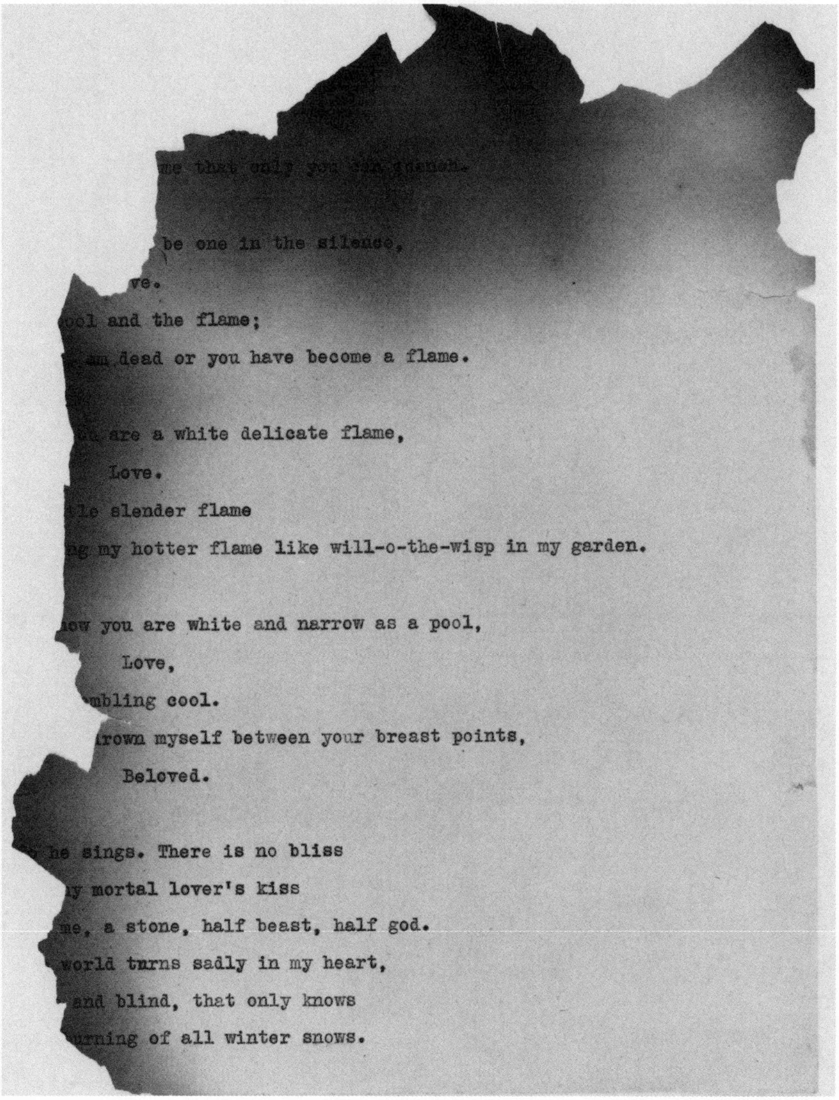

...me that only you can quench.

...be one in the silence,
...ve.
...ol and the flame;
...am dead or you have become a flame.

...are a white delicate flame,
...Love.
...le slender flame
...g my hotter flame like will-o-the-wisp in my garden.

...ow you are white and narrow as a pool,
...Love,
...mbling cool.
...rown myself between your breast points,
...Beloved.

...he sings. There is no bliss
...y mortal lover's kiss
...me, a stone, half beast, half god.
...world turns sadly in my heart,
...nd blind, that only knows
...rning of all winter snows.

Figure 25. Typescript of Second Leaf of Poem Fragment ["azure sea"] (#108b)
(Courtesy Jill Faulkner Summers and the Harry Ransom
Humanities Research Center, The University of Texas, Austin)

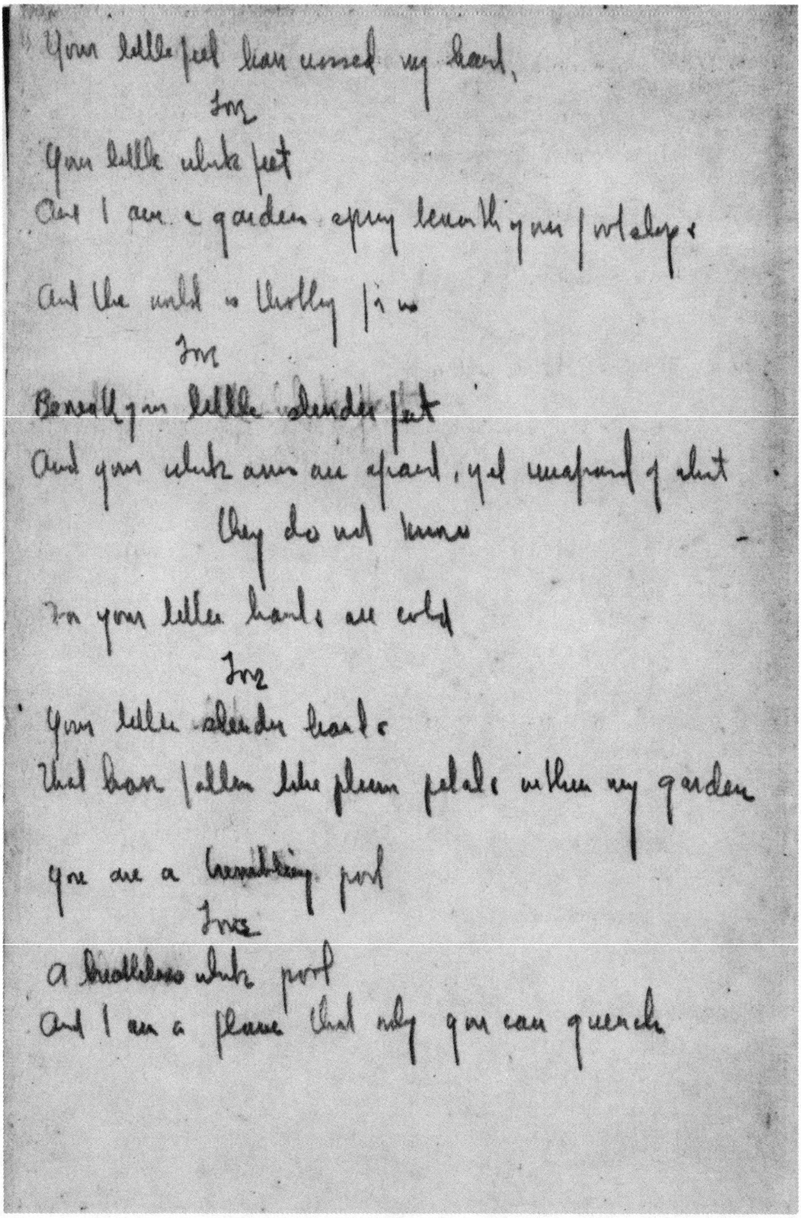

Figure 26. Hodgson Fragment of ["Those cries like scatt[ered silve?]r sails"] (#108c)
(Courtesy Jill Faulkner Summers and the William Faulkner Collection, University of Virginia Library)

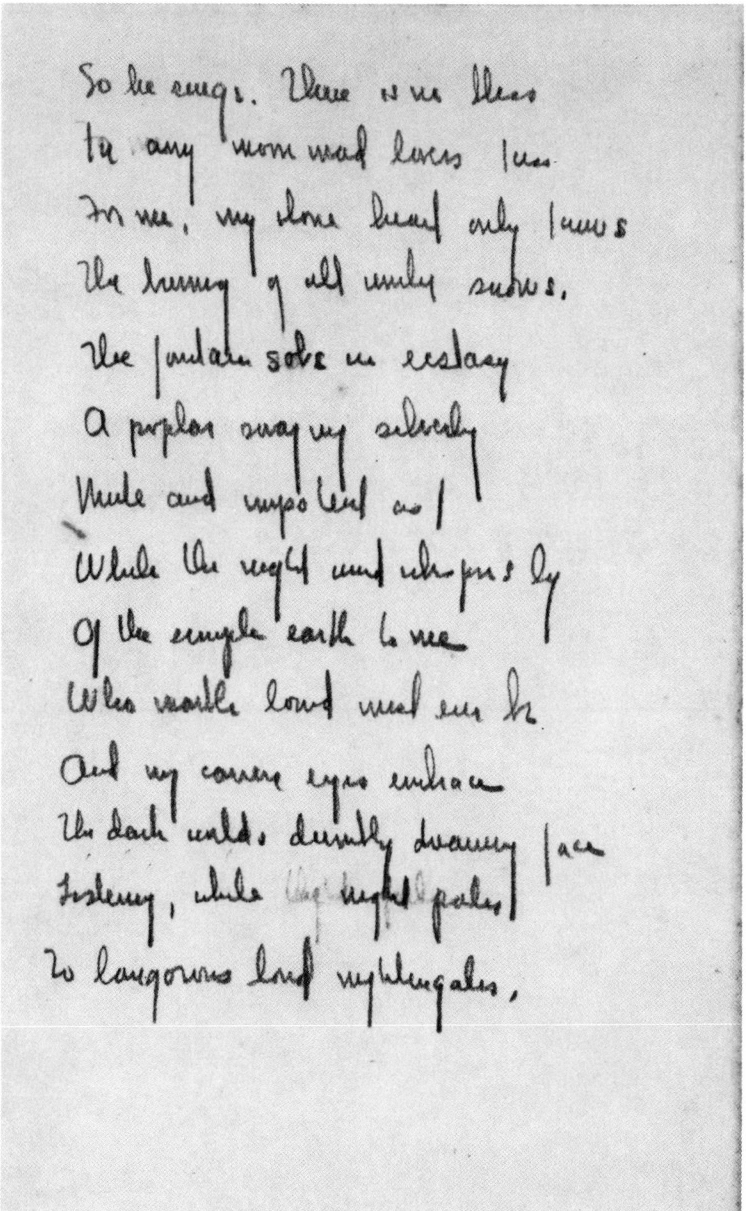

So he sings. There is no bliss
To any more mad lovers less.
For me, my alone heart only knows
The beauty of all emily snows.
The fountain sobs in ecstasy
A poplar swaying silverly
Mute and impotent as I
While the night wind whispers by
Of the simple earth to me
Who... loud must...
And my... eyes embrace
The dark world, dimly dreaming face
Listening, while the night pales
To languorous loud nightingales,

Figure 27. Second Leaf of Hodgson Fragment (#108c)
(Courtesy Jill Faulkner Summers and the William Faulkner Collection, University of Virginia Library)

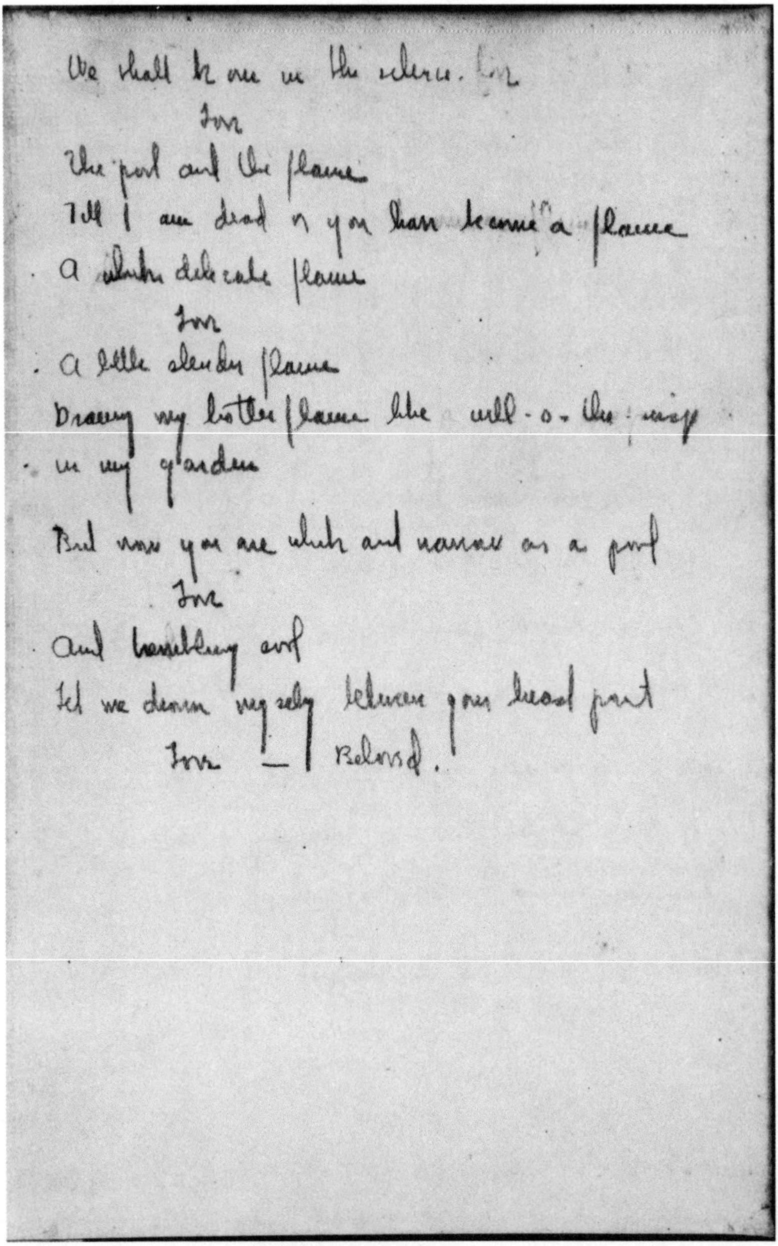

Figure 28. Third Leaf of Hodgson Fragment (#108c)
(Courtesy Jill Faulkner Summers and the William Faulkner Collection, University of Virginia Library)

f. Untitled, 1 p. black ribbon typescript: burned fragment, 17 lines visible, 14 complete; "William Faulkner" typed below poem; TxU.

g. Untitled, 1 p. carbon typescript: burned fragment, 5 quatrains, all but first few letters of last 2 lines complete; first line "Beyond the hill the sun swam downward"; MsU (Wynn, folder 8, #42).

114. "Two Puppets in a Fifth Avenue Win[dow?]"

Transcribed in Polk 1977: xxx–xxxi.

a. "Two Puppets in a Fifth Avenue Win[dow?]," 1 p. black ribbon typescript: burned fragment, 21 lines visible, 12 complete; TxU.

115. "Virginity" [*PV:67]

Con 1 (1 February 1932): 2 and *Wells:* 123 (titled "To a Virgin"). *AGB* XXXIX: 62. *HC/MP:* 119. Manuscript (c) reproduced in *HC 1981:* n.p.

a. "To a Virgin," 1 p. black ribbon typescript; sonnet; identical to *Con* version; ViU (Accession #6074).

b. "[He?]len and Virginity," 1 p. black ribbon typescript: burned fragment, but entire sonnet complete; this draft has 3 ink holograph revisions; at bottom left is typed "At sea, SS West Ivis / 10 July, 1925"; TxU.

c. "Virginity," 1 p. manuscript: sonnet; dated "MAJORCA-JULY-1925"; this is *Helen: A Courtship* VIII; LNT.

116. "Vision in Spring" [*PV:69]

Con 1 (1 February 1932): 1 (titled "Visions in Spring"). Reprinted in *Lillabulero:* 26–27. *VIS:* 1–5.

a. "Vision in Spring," 5 pp. photocopy of carbon typescript: 52 lines; bottoms of pages numbered consecutively "1" through "5"; this is *Vision in Spring* I; ViU (Accession #9817-I).

b. "Vision in Spring," 3 pp. black ribbon typescript on legal-size paper: 13 quatrains, two holograph corrections; "2." penciled above title; text identical to *Con* version except for accent mark over "hushèd" in line 19 of the typescript; this is included in [*Virginia 3*] (#172); ViU (Accession #6074).

c. "Vision in Spring," 3 pp. black ribbon typescript on legal-size paper: 52 lines, all complete; 1 ink holograph correction; TxU.

117. ["When evening shadows grew around"] [*PV:70]

AGB XI: 31. Additional stanza in manuscripts (a) and (e) through (g) transcribed in *Selections:* 26.

    a. Untitled, 1 p. black ribbon typescript on legal-size paper: 5 quatrains; above first line is typed "7"; this is included in [*Virginia 2*] (#171); ViU (Accession #6074).

    b. Untitled, 1 p. typescript: 7 lines and beginning of eighth; MsU (Rowan Oak, box 2, folder 39).

    c. Untitled, 1 p. purple carbon typescript: burned fragment, 14 lines visible, 9 complete; first visible phrase "empty of all save they"; "William Faulkner" typed below poem; TxU.

    d. Untitled, 1 p. purple ribbon typescript: burned fragment, 9 lines visible, 8 complete; first visible phrase "hollowed out with fire"; "William Faulkner" typed below poem; TxU.

    e. Untitled, 1 p. purple ribbon typescript: five quatrains; this is [*Aunt Bama Poems*] IV; *H/B 1982:* 18d; ViU aperture cards (Accession #6074, box 11, #20).

    f. Untitled, 1 p. carbon typescript: burned fragment, parts of 9 lines visible; first visible phrase (from quatrain omitted in *AGB* version) "kissed in the leafy shade"; TxU.

    g. Untitled, 1 p. carbon typescript: burned fragment, parts of 11 lines visible; first visible phrase (from quatrain omitted in *AGB* version) "and kissed in the leafy shade"; TxU.

118. ["When I rose up with morning"]

Transcribed in *Selections:* 25.

    a. Untitled, 1 p. purple ribbon typescript; 3 quatrains; this is [*Aunt Bama Poems*] II; *H/B 1982:* 18b; ViU aperture cards (Accession #6074, box 11, #20).

    b. Untitled, first 3 quatrains of [*Housman*], leaf A; "3" is circled in left margin with penciled remark, "Too much Shropshire Lad"; similar to (a) above with one substantive variant; this is [*Housman*] IV; MsU (Wynn, folder 2, #10).

119. ["When I was young and proud and gay"] [*PV:71]

AGB XIII: 33.

    a. Untitled, 1 p. black ribbon typescript on legal-size paper: 4 quatrains; above first line is typed "8"; this is included in [*Virginia 2*] (#171); ViU (Accession #6074).

b. Untitled, 1 p. typescript: first 11 lines of *AGB* XIII; MsU (Rowan Oak, box 2, folder 43).

c. Untitled, 1 p. black ribbon typescript: burned fragment, 6 lines visible, 3 complete; first visible phrase "Ray and Ralph"; "William Faulkner" typed below poem; TxU.

d. Untitled, 1 p. black ribbon typescript: burned fragment, parts of 11 lines visible; first visible phrase "such a page to spell"; black ink arrows in margins; TxU.

e. Untitled, 1 p. purple ribbon typescript: burned fragment, 11 lines visible, 8 complete; first visible phrase "as well"; TxU.

f. Untitled, 1 p. black ribbon typescript: burned fragment, parts of 11 lines visible; first visible phrase "such a page to spell"; TxU.

g. Untitled, 1 p. black ribbon typescript: burned fragment, 12 lines visible, 8 complete; first visible word "spell"; Roman numeral "X." typed below last line; penciled Arabic numeral "1" circled beside last line; TxU.

h. Untitled, 1 p. purple carbon typescript: burned fragment, 12 lines visible, 8 complete; first visible phrase "to spread it"; "William Faulkner" typed below poem; TxU.

i. Untitled, 1 p. purple ribbon typescript: four quatrains; slightly revised when publshed as *AGB* XIII; this is [*Aunt Bama Poems*] V; *H/B 1982* 18f; ViU aperture cards (Accession #6074, box 11, #20).

120. ["Who sprang to be his land's defense"] [*PV:74]

Epigraph to part 2 of chapter I, *Soldiers' Pay:* 23. Five additional lines appear on p. 25.

a. Untitled, *Soldiers' Pay* typescript, f. 25: 9 lines; first 3, which do not appear in the published text, are canceled; MsU.

b. Untitled, *Soldiers' Pay* typescript; the first 3 lines of this epigraph are exactly like those in the MsU typescript; there are minor differences in the other 6 lines; NN-B.

c. Untitled, *Soldiers' Pay* typescript; this inserted sheet contains 4 lines of the epigraph, incomplete; NN-B.

121. "Wild Geese" [*PV:72]

NR 74 (12 April 1933): 253 (titled "Over the World's Rim"). *AGB* XXVIII: 51. *HC/MP:* 152. Typescript (c) reproduced in *MP 1979:* 19.

a. "Wild Geese," 1 p. black ribbon typescript: burned fragment, 4 quatrains visible, all but last quatrain complete; TxU.

b. "Wild Geese," 1 p. black ribbon typescript: burned fragment, parts of 17 lines visible; TxU.
c. "IV. / Wild Geese," 1 p. carbon typescript: 4 quatrains; "William Faulkner" at bottom in type and holograph; this is Brodsky's *Mississippi Poems* IV; *H/B 1982:* 45d.
d. "IV. / Wild Geese," 1 p. ribbon typescript: 4 quatrains; "William Faulkner" typed at bottom; this is *Mississippi Poems* IV; MsU (Wynn, folder 7, #36).

122. "Winter Is Gone" [*PV:73]

Con 1 (1 February 1932): 2 and *Wells:* 124. *Lillabulero:* 25.

a. Untitled, 1 p. black ribbon typescript on legal-size paper: 4 quatrains; first line "Winter is gone, snow but an old wives tale:"; "3." typed above first line; this is included in [*Virginia 2*] (#171); ViU (Accession #6074).
b. Untitled, 1 p. black ribbon typescript: burned, but all 16 lines complete; first line "Winter is gone, snow but an old-wives' tale"; "William Faulkner" typed at bottom; TxU.
c. Untitled, 7 burned carbons in various stages of disintegration; TxU.

123. "The World and Pierrot. A Nocturne" [*PV:45]

VIS: 10–29. Part 2 of this 18-page poem (lines 29–50 with 11 variants) appeared in *OM:* 214–15, titled "Nocturne." The *OM* version, with author's illustration, reproduced in *EPP:* 82–83, *Meriwether:* figure 2, *Origins:* 144, and *Stylization:* 35 (figure 32).

a. "The World and Pierrot. A Nocturne," 18 pp. photocopy of carbon typescript: 224 lines; bottoms of pages numbered consecutively "10" through "29"; this is *Vision in Spring* III; ViU (Accession #9817-I).

124. ["You see here in this leaden tenement"]

Transcribed and discussed in *Stylization:* 113.

a. Untitled, 1 p. black ribbon typescript: sonnet; TxU.

125. ["Young Richard, striding toward town"] [*PV:75]

AGB XII: 32.

a. Untitled, 1 p. black ribbon typescript on legal-size paper: 4 quatrains; above first line is typed "6."; this is included in [*Virginia 2*] (#171); ViU (Accession #6074).

b. Untitled, 1 p. carbon typescript: burned fragment, ends of 6 lines visible; first visible phrase "[l?]apped him close"; TxU.
c. Untitled, 1 p. carbon typescript: burned fragment, 16 lines visible, 6 complete; first visible phrase "toward town"; TxU.
d. Untitled, 1 p. black ribbon typescript: burned fragment, ends of 9 lines visible; first visible phrase "him close"; TxU.
e. Untitled, 1 p. typescript: burned but all 16 lines are complete; MsU (Wynn, folder 8, #43).

2

Unpublished Verse

126. ["Admonishes his heart"] [*UV:2]

Final sestet of this poem appears in *Blotner 1974:* 544. Untitled, 1 p. typescript: sonnet; 1 line under title canceled; 3 ink holograph corrections; dated "14 March 1927"; MsU (Rowan Oak, box 2, folder 43).

127. "Blue Hills" [*UV:5]

 a. "Blue Hills," 1 p. black ribbon typescript: burned fragment, 16 lines in quatrains visible, 12 complete; "[Fa?]ulkner" typed at top; TxU.
 b. "[Blue?] Hills," 1 p. black ribbon typescript: burned fragment, 4 quatrains visible, 8 lines complete; 6 holograph corrections which have been incorporated into (a) above; dateline "[Wes?]t Ivis" at bottom; TxU.

128. ["But now I'm dead: no wine is sweet to me"] [*UV:6]

Untitled, 1 p. black ink manuscript: 12 lines, with 11 lines of revised draft below; on other side is penciled holograph draft of "The Poet's Confession is Replied To" (#147); NN-B.

129. "Cathedral in Rain" [*UV:7]

1 p. carbon typescript: burned fragment, 15 lines visible, first 13 complete; 2 ink holograph corrections; TxU.

130. ["Dead, 0 dead, the sorrow loved of spring"] [*UV:9]

Untitled, 1 p. typescript: 2 seven-line stanzas; beneath the poem are penciled scrawlings (child's?); on other side is poem beginning "Where I am dead the clover loved of bees" (#158); NN-B.

131. ["Diana, put by your bow and spear"] [*UF:60]

Together the following typescripts form a complete draft of the poem.

    a. Untitled, final 15 lines of [*Housman*], leaf D: 14 lines complete; "XII" above first line; this is [*Housman*] XII; MsU (Wynn, folder 2, #13).

    b. Untitled, 1 p. purple ribbon typescript: burned fragment, 2 quatrains visible and complete; first visible line "Your bonds are strong as steel, but soft"; beneath final line is typed "William Faulkner"; TxU.

132. "Don Manuel" [*UV:10]

1 p. typescript: burned fragment, 23 lines visible, 20 complete, CtY.

133. "Hallowe'en" [*UV:14]

6 pp. typescript: burned fragments, 110 lines visible, 89 complete; TxU.

134. ["I cannot die nor hope to find death such"] [*UV:17]

Untitled, 1 p. penciled manuscript: 14 lines, 1 canceled; below this are 8 more lines beginning "Now you are dead and all sweet things must pass" (#144); beside it are 2 illegible lines which appear to be the rough draft of another poem; on other side is unsigned and undated 3-line typescript fragment from one of Faulkner's *New Orleans Sketches,* "The Kid learns"; NN-B.

135. ["I knew love once, I knew brief despair"]

Untitled, 1 p. typescript: 4 quatrains visible and complete; burned fragment but seems complete; this is not "Knew I Love Once" (#57); MsU (Wynn, folder 5, #28).

136. ["In evening, when raucous crows flap blackly home to [?]"]

Untitled, 1 p. typescript: burned fragment, 3 six-line stanzas visible, all but first line complete; MsU (Wynn, folder 3, #17).

137. "The London Mail" [*UF: 27, 54]

The following typescripts form a complete draft of the poem.

    a. "The London Mail," 2 pp. typescript: burned fragment, 6 quatrains visible on first page, all but last complete; 2 quatrains visible and complete on second page; "2" and "3" circled in left margin below poem; MsU (Wynn, folder 4, #22–23).

b. Untitled, 1 p. black ribbon typescript: burned fragment, parts of 12 lines visible; first visible phrase "winds and rains"; includes parts of first 4 quatrains of (a) above; TxU.

c. Untitled, 1 p. purple carbon typescript: burned fragment, 3 quatrains visible, 11 lines complete; first visible phrase "guard's far horn"; parts of third through fifth quatrains of (a) above; TxU.

d. Untitled, 1 p. black ribbon typescript: burned fragment, 12 lines visible, 4 complete; first visible word "lad"; "[Faul?]k[ne?]r" typed at end of poem; corresponds with seventh quatrain and parts of sixth and eighth quatrains of (a) above; TxU.

e. Untitled, 1 p. purple carbon typescript: burned fragment, 4 lines visible, 2 complete; first visible phrase "three merry men"; "William Faulkner" typed at bottom of page; corresponds with last 4 lines of (a) above; TxU.

138. "Mary Magdalen"

Typescripts (a) and (c) form a complete draft of the poem.

a. Untitled, 1 p. black ribbon typescript: burned fragment, 19 lines arranged in quatrains visible, 16 lines complete; first visible phrase "[The harbor make?]s [th?]e bed-room glary"; "William Faulkner" typed at bottom; TxU.

b. Untitled, 1 p. carbon typescript: burned fragment, 14 lines in quatrains visible, 6 complete; "William Faulkner." typed at bottom; first visible phrase "head,—she mutters"; not a duplicate of (a) above, but no substantive variants; TxU.

c. "Mary Magdalen," 1 p. typescript: burned fragment, 5 quatrains visible, all but last line complete; MsU (Wynn, folder 4, #19).

139. ["Never is living quiet"]

a. Untitled, last, incomplete stanza on [*Housman*] leaf A and probably first two quatrains of leaf B (see #168); penciled in left margin of leaf B after second quatrain are "3," "3," and perhaps "4"; this is [*Housman*] V; MsU (Wynn, folder 2, #10–11).

b. Untitled, 1 p. typescript: burned fragment, 6 lines visible, 4 complete; first visible phrase "with fate"; "William Faulkner" typed below poem; TxU.

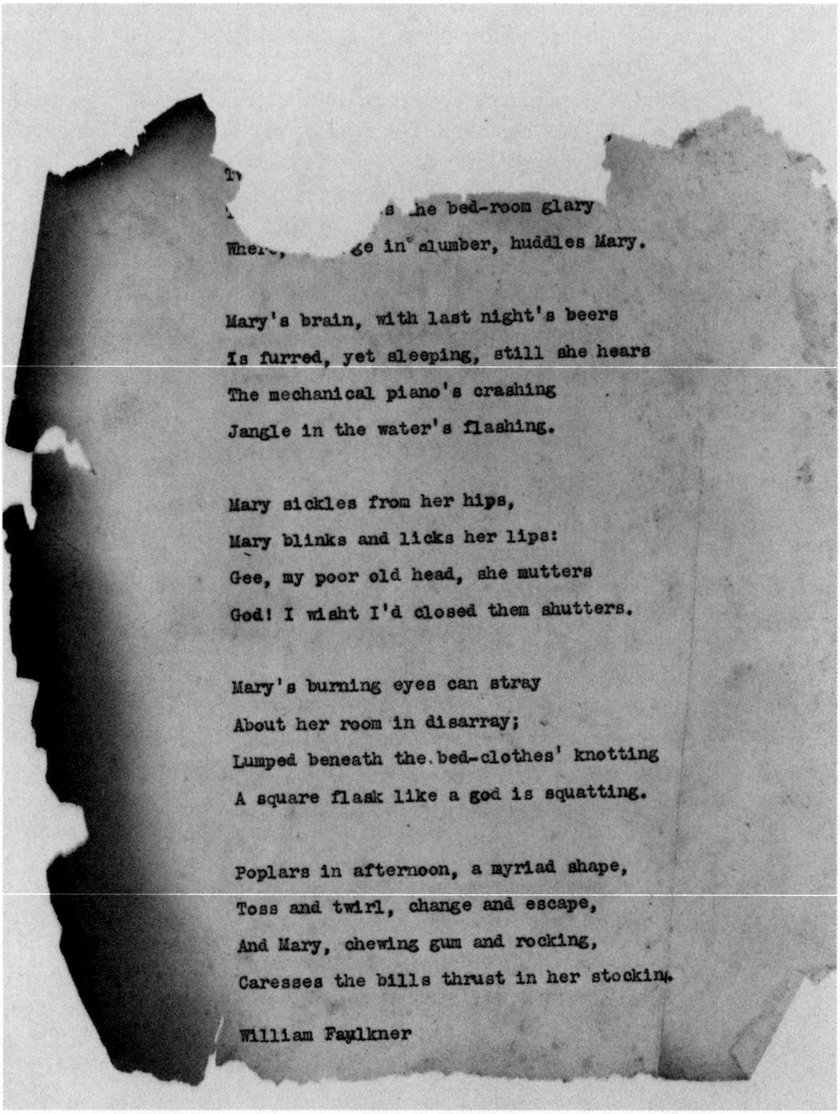

...........s .he bed-room glary
Where, ...ge in slumber, huddles Mary.

Mary's brain, with last night's beers
Is furred, yet sleeping, still she hears
The mechanical piano's crashing
Jangle in the water's flashing.

Mary sickles from her hips,
Mary blinks and licks her lips:
Gee, my poor old head, she mutters
God! I wisht I'd closed them shutters.

Mary's burning eyes can stray
About her room in disarray;
Lumped beneath the.bed-clothes' knotting
A square flask like a god is squatting.

Poplars in afternoon, a myriad shape,
Toss and twirl, change and escape,
And Mary, chewing gum and rocking,
Caresses the bills thrust in her stocking.

William Faulkner

Figure 29. Typescript Fragment of "Mary Magdalen" (#138a)
(Courtesy Jill Faulkner Summers and the Harry Ransom
Humanities Research Center, The University of Texas, Austin)

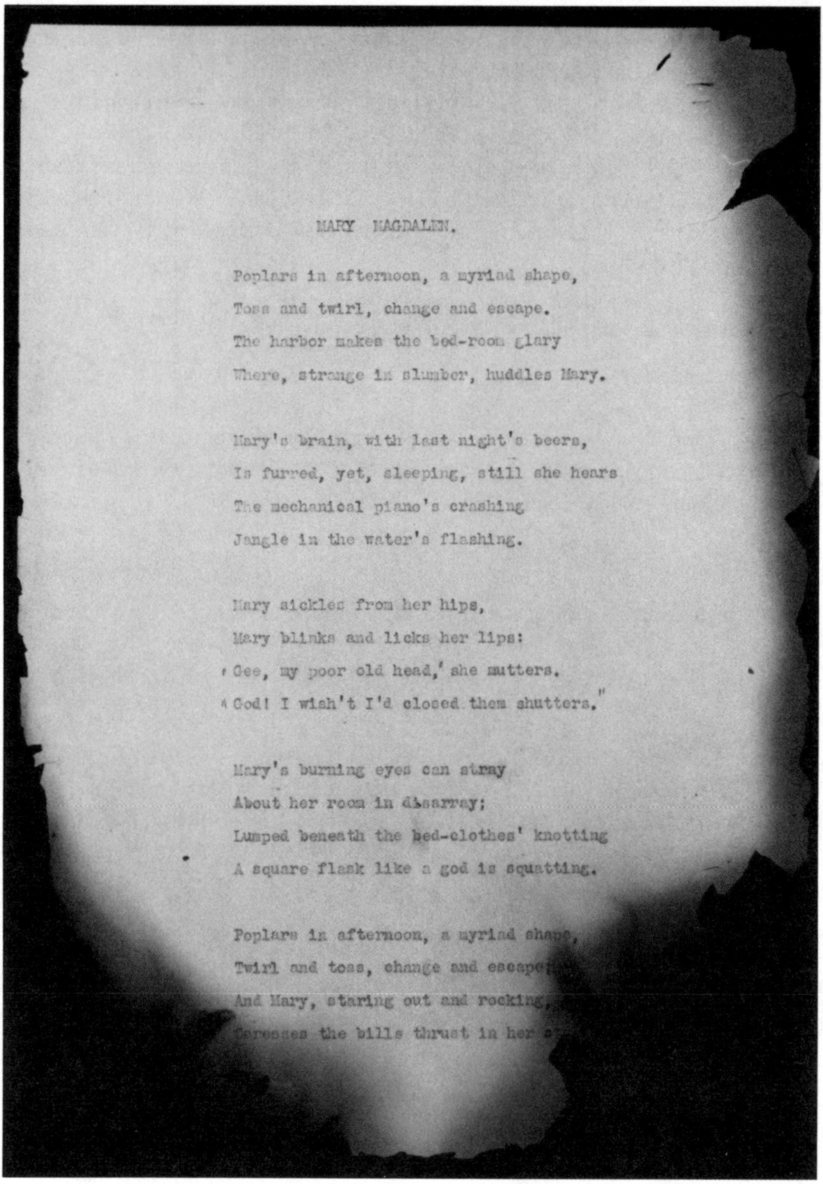

MARY MAGDALEN.

Poplars in afternoon, a myriad shape,
Toss and twirl, change and escape.
The harbor makes the bed-room glary
Where, strange in slumber, huddles Mary.

Mary's brain, with last night's beers,
Is furred, yet, sleeping, still she hears
The mechanical piano's crashing
Jangle in the water's flashing.

Mary sickles from her hips,
Mary blinks and licks her lips:
'Gee, my poor old head,' she mutters.
'God! I wish't I'd closed them shutters.'

Mary's burning eyes can stray
About her room in disarray;
Lumped beneath the bed-clothes' knotting
A square flask like a god is squatting.

Poplars in afternoon, a myriad shape,
Twirl and toss, change and escape.
And Mary, staring out and rocking,
caresses the bills thrust in her

Figure 30.   Typescript Complementary Fragment of "Mary Magdalen"
(#138c)
*(Courtesy Jill Faulkner Summers and the University of
Mississippi Library)*

140. "New Orleans" [*UV:21]

    a. "New Orleans," 1 p. black ribbon typescript: sonnet; last line is scanned in pencil; TxU.

    b. "New Orleans," 1 p. carbon typescript (not of (a) above): burned but complete; "2." typed above title; TxU.

    c. "New Orleans," 1 p. typescript: burned but complete sonnet divided as 2 quatrains and sestet; black ink holograph "William Faulkner / Oxford / 30 October 1924" written below poem; MsU (Wynn, folder 5, #25).

141. ["No moon will lighter sleep within these leaves"] [*UV:22]

    a. Untitled, 1 p. typescript: sonnet, MsU (Rowan Oak, box 2, folder 39).

    b. Untitled, 1 p. pencil holograph draft: burned fragment, 19 lines visible, 18 complete; on other side appear to be notes for a short story; MsU (Wynn, folder 9).

142. "Nostalgia" [*UV:23]

1 p. ink manuscript: rough draft of 11-line poem beginning "When down the hills of evening slowly, sun"; followed by 6 lines of revision; on other side is untitled rough draft of "Knew I Love Once" (#57c); NN-B.

143. "Nostalgia"

1 p. typescript: 4 quatrains visible and complete; typed at bottom of page, "William Faulkner / Capri, 1925" (originally "1924"); this is a different poem from #142, which is also entitled "Nostalgia"; MsU (Wynn, folder 5, #27).

144. ["Now you are dead, and all sweet things must pass"]

Untitled, 1 p. penciled manuscript: 2 quatrains with cancelations throughout; appears below 14-line poem beginning "I cannot die nor hope to find death such" (#134); also on page are 2 illegible lines which appear to be a different poem; on other side is 3-line typescript fragment from Faulkner's *New Orleans Sketches:* "The kid learns"; NN-B.

145. ["O Thyrsis, he's the lover"]

Untitled, fourth quatrain of [*Housman*], leaf C and first 2 quatrains of leaf D (see #168); "XI" above first line; "3" and "3" circled in margin of leaf D at end of poem; this is [*Housman*] XI; MsU (Wynn, folder 2, #12–13).

146. "Old Ace"

Lines from and discussion of this poem appear in *Blotner 1974:* 1131–32.

    a. Untitled, 3 pp. typescript of a prose poem: 60 lines, 6 stanzas; first line "They looked down at him across the rigid thumbs-up"; "William Faulkner" typed in upper left-hand corner; ViU (Accession #9817-b).

    b. Untitled, 1 p. typescript letter: contains revisions for "Old Ace"; dated "26 November 1942"; ViU (Accession #8969, box 1: "Ober-Faulkner Material").

147. "The Poet's Confession is Replied to" [*UV:27 and 42]

    a. "The Poet's Confession is Replied to," 1 p. manuscript: 22 lines; the poem is written as the poet's dialogue with 3 female speakers—he has the final line; NN-B.

    b. Untitled, 1 p. manuscript: 13 lines beginning "You and your verse! Do you then believe / I gave my red mouth's kiss for an empty line"; these lines are drafts of first 9 lines of (a) above; further down the page is 3-line fragment beginning "Slanting the broken moon to planes of light" (#198); NN-B.

148. "Queen Sappho" [*UF:42]

    a. Untitled, 1 p. purple carbon typescript: burned fragment, last 3 quatrains visible, last 2 quatrains complete; first complete line (fifth line) "Queen Sappho, in the starry dusk"; "William Faulkner" typed at bottom; TxU.

    b. "Queen Sappho," 1 p. typescript: burned fragment, 4 quatrains visible and complete; "To V. M." in black ink holograph under title; "3" circled in left margin below poem; MsU (Wynn, folder 5, #26).

149. "The River" [*UV:29]

1 p. black ribbon typescript: burned fragment, 17 lines visible in quatrains, 3 quatrains complete; TxU.

150. "Scaramouch"

2 pp. typescript: burned fragment, first page has 6 quatrains visible, all but sixth complete; second page has 4 quatrains visible and complete; "3" and "3" circled in margin below poem; MsU (Wynn, folder 4, #20–21).

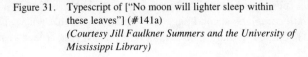

No moon will lighter sleep within these leaves
Because the mouth you kissed grows cold and keen,
Having forgot thy mouth. Have these hands seen
Thy faultless cuirass and subtle greaves

In the dark? This the mouth that hears
Orisons in thy young breast's rounded nave'
Within thy thighs let me find death and grave
Than wake to heir me brief and bitter tears.

O hold me, love; let us kiss close, nor see
That living, and not death, must come between;
O bind me fast in thy soft hair, lest we
See each the stranger we have always been.

Let this one heart-break! the sorrow's not
In heart-break: 'tis heart-break's so soon forgot.

Figure 31. Typescript of ["No moon will lighter sleep within
these leaves"] (#141a)
*(Courtesy Jill Faulkner Summers and the University of
Mississippi Library)*

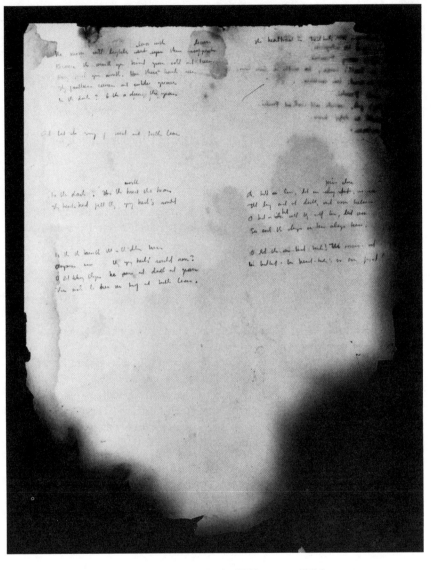

Figure 32.   Pencil Holograph Draft of ["No moon will lighter
sleep within these leaves"] (#141b)
*(Courtesy Jill Faulkner Summers and the University of
Mississippi Library)*

151. "The Shepherd's Love" [*UV:31]

 a. "The Shepherd's Love," 1 p. black ribbon typescript on legal-size paper: 4 five-line stanzas; first line "O come sweet love, and let us keep"; although unnumbered, this is included in [*Virginia 3*] (#172); ViU (Accession #6074).

 b. "The Shepherd's Love," 1 p. carbon typescript: burned fragment, 20 lines in five-line stanzas, 16 lines complete; TxU.

 c. Untitled, 1 p. typescript: burned fragment: ends of 13 lines visible; first visible word "still"; TxU.

 d. Untitled, 1 p. carbon typescript: burned fragment, ends of 12 lines visible; first visible word "still"; TxU.

152. "Sunset"

 1 p. typescript: burned fragment, 2 quatrains visible and complete; "For magazines" penciled at top of page and "2" and "3" circled below poem; MsU (Wynn, folder 3, #18).

153. ["Sweet will it be to us who sleep"] [*UV:32]

 a. Untitled, 1 p. black ribbon typescript: 3 quatrains; ViU (Accession #6074).

 b. Untitled, 1 p. carbon typescript: burned fragment, 12 lines visible, 11 complete; TxU.

 c. Untitled, 1 p. carbon typescript: burned, but all 3 quatrains are complete; TxU.

 d. Untitled, 1 p. carbon typescript: burned fragment, parts of 11 lines visible, first visible phrase "that creep"; TxU.

 e. Untitled, 1 p. carbon typescript: burned fragment, parts of 11 lines visible; first visible phrase "that creep"; TxU.

154. ["Wake Me Not, 0 April, Now I'm Old"] [*UV:37]

 a. Untitled, 1 p. carbon typescript: burned but complete sonnet; Arabic numeral "1." typed at top; TxU.

 b. Untitled, 1 p. black ribbon typescript: burned but complete sonnet; penciled Arabic numeral "1" circled beside final 2 lines; TxU.

155. ["What'll I do today?"] [*UV:38]

 Last 11 lines transcribed in *Blotner 1974:* 454.

 Untitled, 1 p. typescript: 17 lines, 4 cancelations; dated "Paris 27 Aug 1925"; heavily revised draft; MsU (Rowan Oak, box 2, folder 42).

156. "Wheat" [*UV:39]

    1 p. black ink manuscript: burned but 19 heavily revised lines complete, 4 lines canceled; below these lines is what appears to be another poem titled "[The Pool?]" and parts of 3 lines; TxU.

157. ["When I am gone—and I shall go before you—"]

    Untitled, 1 p. black ribbon typescript: sonnet; TxU.

158. ["Where I am dead the clover loved of bees"] [*UV:41]

    Final quatrain of manuscript (a) transcribed in *Blotner 1974: 397*.

    a. Untitled, 1 p. black ribbon typescript: 4 quatrains, 1 ink holograph correction; the second stanza has been canceled; at the bottom is typed "William Faulkner / New Orleans / 10 February 1925"; ViU (Accession #6074).

    b. Untitled, 1 p. typescript: 4 quatrains; ink holograph corrections in second and fourth stanzas; dated "New Orleans / 9 February 1925"; on other side is 14-line poem beginning "Dead, O dead, the sorrow loved of Spring" (#130); NN-B.

159. ["You have seen music, heard"]

    Untitled, 1 p. typescript: 6 lines; this poem bears a remarkable resemblance to a poem written for and quoted by Meta Carpenter Wilde (see #51)—*Bonner* (entry #52) states that this typescript is "possibly related to Helen Baird"; LNT.

3

Published and Unpublished Sequences and Sequence Fragments

160. [*Aunt Bama Poems*]

Unpublished ribbon typescript. Gift which LDB says consisted originally of 15 poems for Faulkner's paternal great-aunt, Alabama Falkner (Mrs. Walter B.) McLean. Brodsky now owns 12 of these poems which are listed below. ViU owns the remaining 3. 7 poems are numbered with Roman numerals I through VII; the other 5 are titled. The numbered sequence appears on four leaves (recto only) of 14-by-8½-inch water-marked paper. Leaf 1 includes poems I and II; leaf 2 includes poem III and the first two stanzas of poem IV; leaf 3 includes the remainder of IV and all of V; leaf 4 includes poems VI and VII. The remaining 5 titled poems, arbitrarily numbered below as (i) through (v), appear on separate leaves. *H/B 1982:* 18 describes this group of poems (which, v excepted, is also available on ViU microfilm) and claims that the three others, "Aubade" (#9), "Hymn" (#48), and "Pastoral" (#80), which are owned by ViU, were also originally included in this grouping. The contents of Brodsky's [*Aunt Bama Poems*] are listed below. See published verse entries for other manuscripts and for publications of each poem. ViU aperture cards (Accession #6074, series VIII, box 11, #20).

I. ["The sun lay long upon the hills"]. See #106.
II. ["When I rose up with morning"]. See #118.
III. ["Turn again, Dick Whittington"]. See #112.
IV. ["When evening shadows grew around"]. See #117.
V. ["I give the world to love you"]. See #50.
VI. ["When I was young and proud and gay"]. See #119.
VII. ["Green grow the rushes O"]. See #40.
[i.] ["The black bird swung in the white rose tree"]. See #14.
[ii.] "An Old Man Says." See "I Will Not Weep for Youth" (#53).
[iii.] "Eunice." See #33.

[iv.] "Elder Watson in Heaven." See #29.
[v.] "Pierrot, Sitting Beside the Body of Colombine, suddenly Sees / Himself in a Mirror." See #83.

161. [*Estelle Poems*]

Reproduced in *Stylization:* 87 (figures 83–85). 3 ink holograph poems on a single white sheet of paper folded into 4 parts; pen and ink illustration of nymph and satyr on back; see *Blotner 1974:* 195 for description of original and discussion; location of original unknown; original photocopy JFS; copy available ViU (Accession #9817-I). Contents of this booklet listed below. See individual entries for each poem.

[I.] "A Song." See #102.
[II.] "Dawn." See #23.
[III.] "An Orchid." See #79.

162. *A Green Bough* [*PV:25]

For publications of this 44-poem volume, see short title listing, *AGB*. As all extant typescripts are printers' copies, I list contents of the published version below by Roman numeral and first line. Other publications, typescripts, and manuscripts of each poem are entered separately, either by first line (if untitled) or by title from other versions (see cross-references in entries below). [*PV:25]

a. [*A Green Bough*], 70 pp. (5 blank) typescript with holograph corrections; this is setting copy for 1933 edition; in the upper left corner of the first page is written in a hand other than the author's, "The Green Bough / Harrison Smith and Robert Haas"; poems are not numbered, but many are titled in Faulkner's hand; TxU.
b. [*A Green Bough*], 14 galley proofs with ink holograph corrections; at the top of each galley is stamped a notation that proof is to be returned by "Jan 27 1933"; Roman numerals are inserted and all titles deleted; at end, in ink holograph, "My idea was not to have a blank page between the poems; merely to start each new poem on a fresh *page*"; TxU.

I. ["We sit drinking tea"], pp. 7–11. See "The Lilacs" (#63).
II. ["Laxly reclining, he watches the firelight going"], pp. 12–15. See "Marriage" (#69).
III. ["The cave was ribbed with dark. Then seven lights"], pp. 16–19. See "Floyd Collins" (#37).
IV. ["and let"], pp. 20–21. See "Guidebook" (#41).

V. ["There is no shortening-breasted nymph to shake"], pp. 22–23. See "Philosophy" (#82).

VI. ["Man comes, man goes, and leaves behind"], p. 24. See "Man Comes, Man Goes" (#66).

VII. ["Trumpets of sun to silence fall"], pp. 25–26. See "Night Piece" (#74).

VIII. ["He furrows the brown earth, doubly sweet"], pp. 27–28. See #43.

IX. ["The sun lies long upon the hills"], p. 29. See #106.

X. ["Beyond the hill the sun swam downward"], p. 30. See "Twilight" (#113).

XI. ["When evening shadows grew around"], p. 31. See #117.

XII. ["Young Richard, striding toward town"], p. 32. See #125.

XIII. ["When I was young and proud and gay"], p. 33. See #119.

XIV. ["His mother said: I'll make him"], pp. 34–35. See "The Gallows" (#38).

XV. ["Bonny earth and bonny sky"], p. 36. See #15.

XVI. ["Behold me, in my feathered cap and doublet"], pp. 37–38. See "Puck and Death" (#89).

XVII. ["o atthis"], p. 39. See "On Seeing the Winged Victory for the First Time" (#78).

XVIII. ["Once upon an adolescent hill"], p. 40. See "A Dead Pilot" (#25).

XIX. ["Green is the water, green"], p. 41. See "Drowning" (#27).

XX. ["Here he stands, while eternal evening falls"], p. 42. See "Orpheus" (#80).

XXI. ["What sorrow, knights and gentles? scroll and"], p. 43. See "Roland" (#94).

XXII. ["I see your face through the twilight of my mind"], p. 44. See #52.

XXIII. ["Somewhere a moon will bloom and find me not"], p. 45. As this also appeared as the last strophe of *HC* XIV, see ["Somewhere is spring with green and simple gold"], #101.

XXIV. ["How canst thou be chaste, when lonely nights"], p. 46. See #47.

XXV. ["Was this the dream"?] p. 47. See "Eros" (#30).

XXVI. ["Still, and look down, look down"], p. 48. See "Eros After" (#31).

XXVII. ["The Raven bleak and Philomel"], pp. 49–50. See #92.

XXVIII. ["Over the world's rim, drawing bland November"], p. 51. See "Wild Geese" (#121).

Figure 33. "A Song" from [Estelle Poems] with Illustration by Faulkner (#161) (Courtesy Jill Faulkner Summers and the William Faulkner Collection, University of Virginia Library)

A SONG

It is all in vain to implore me,
To let not her image beguile,
For her face is ever before me —
And her smile.

Even though she choose to ignore me,
And all love of me to deny,
There is nought then behind or before me —
I can die.

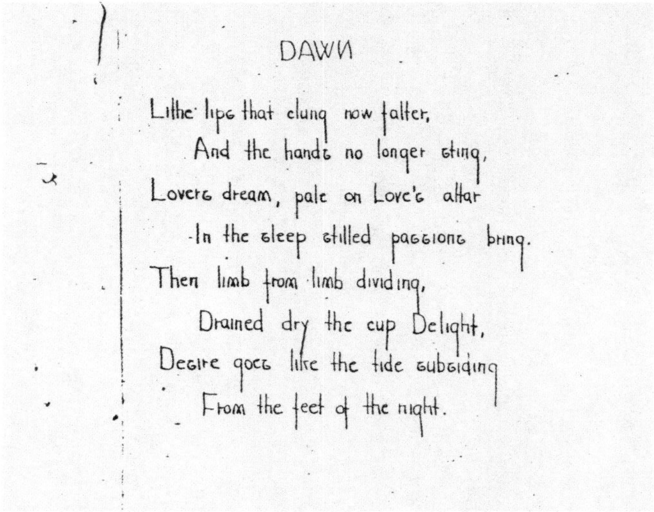

DAWN

Lithe lips that clung now falter,
And the hands no longer sting,
Lovers dream, pale on Love's altar
In the sleep stilled passions bring.
Then limb from limb dividing,
Drained dry the cup Delight,
Desire goes like the tide subsiding
From the feet of the night.

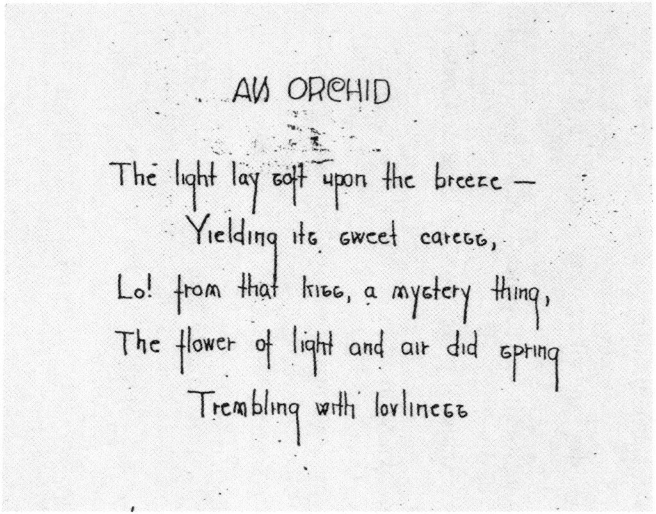

AN ORCHID

The light lay soft upon the breeze —
Yielding its sweet caress,
Lo! from that kiss, a mystery thing,
The flower of light and air did spring
Trembling with lovliness

Figure 34. "Dawn" and "An Orchid" from [*Estelle Poems*] (#161)
(Courtesy Jill Faulkner Summers and the William Faulkner Collection, University of Virginia Library)

XXIX. ["As to an ancient music's hidden fall"], p. 52. See "Pregnacy" [*sic*] (#87).

XXX. ["Gray the day, and all the year is cold"], p. 53. See "November 11" (#75).

XXXI. ["He winnowed it with bayonets"], p. 54. See "The Husbandman" (#48).

XXXII. ["look, cynthia"], p. 55. See "La Lune ne Grade Aucune Rancune" (#65).

XXXIII. ["Did I know love once? Was it love or grief"], p. 56. See "Knew I Love Once" (#57).

XXXIV. ["The ship of night, with twilightcolored sails"], p. 57. See "The Ship of Night" (#100).

XXXV. ["The courtesan is dead, for all her subtle ways"], p. 58. See "Indian Summer" (#54).

XXXVI. ["Gusty trees windily lean on green"], p. 59. See "Spring" (#103).

XXXVII. ["The race's splendor lifts her lip, exposes"], p. 60. See "The Race's Splendor" (#90).

XXXVIII. ["Lips that of thy weary all seem weariest"], p. 61. See "Hermaphroditus" (#45).

XXXIX. ["Like to the tree that, young, reluctant yet"], p. 62. See "Virginity" (#115).

XL. ["Lady, unawares still bride of sleep"], p. 63. See "She Lies Sleeping" (#99).

XLI. ["Her unripe shallow breast is green among"], p. 64. See "Old Satyr" (#77).

XLII. ["Beneath the apple tree Eve's tortured shape"], p. 65. See "March" (#67).

XLIII. ["let's see I'll say—between two brief balloons"], p. 66. See "Proposal" (#88).

XLIV. ["If there be grief, then let it be but rain"], p. 67. See "Mississippi Hills: My Epitaph" (#70).

163. *Helen: A Courtship*

For published editions, see short title listing *HC/MP 1981* and *HC 1981*. 16 poems in hand-bound ink holograph booklet. A gift to Helen Baird, dated "Oxford, Mississippi, June, 1926." 1 dedicatory poem followed by 15 sonnets, sequenced by Roman numerals, each appearing on the recto of an individual page. See *Bonner:* 148 for complete description of the booklet; the following poems appear in this sequence—for other manuscripts, typescripts, and/or publications, see individual entries for each poem; LNT.

"To Helen, Swimming." See #111.

I. "Bill." See #13.

II. ["Beneath the apple tree Eve's tortured shape"]. See "March" (#67).

III. ["With laggard March, a faun whose stampings ring"]. See "The Faun" (#35).

IV. ["Her unripe shallow breast is green among"]. See "Old Satyr" (#77).

V. "Proposal." See #88.

VI. ["My health? My health's a fevered loud distress"]. See #72.

VII. ["The Centaur takes the sun to skull his lyre"]. See "Helen and the Centaur" (#44).

VIII. "Virginity." See #115.

IX. ["Goodbye, goodnight: goodnight were more than fair"]. See #39.

X. ["Ah no, ah no: my sleep is mine, mine own"]. See #5.

XI. ["Let that sleep have no end, which brings me waking"]. See #61.

XII. ["Let there be no farewell shaped between"]. See #62.

XIII. ["O I have heard the evening trumpeted"]. See "Leaving Her" (#60).

XIV. ["Somewhere is spring with green and simple gold"]. See #101.

XV. ["Knew I love once? Was it love or grief"]. See "Knew I Love Once" (#57).

164. *The Lilacs*

Unpublished. 36-page hand-lettered and illustrated booklet containing 13 poems. Assembled by Faulkner and presented to Phil Stone, to whom it is dedicated. *The Lilacs* manuscript is owned by L. D. Brodsky (*H/B 1982:* 26). Following is Brodsky's description of the contents. Poems that exist in other manuscripts and publications have individual entries in this bibliography (see cross-references). Those that appear only in *The Lilacs* are described below.

[1] Title page

[2] Dedication page reading: ". . .Phil Stone / . . . book is / . . . affectionately dedicated: / . . . quand il fait Sombre.' / . . . Jan. 1 1920."

[3] Blank page

[4] Watercolor of woman

[5–14] "The Lilacs." See #63.

[15–16] "Ca[thay?]." See "Cathay" (#16).

[17] Untitled, first visible phrase "The dawn herself [?]." See "To a Co-ed" (#109).

[18] Untitled, 3 lines visible; unidentified poem; key visible phrase "[?]pering candles."

[19] Untitled, first line "O Atthis." See "On Seeing the Winged Victory for the First Time" (#78).

[20] "[?] Living," burned fragment: parts of 9 lines visible.

[21–23] "L'Apres-Midi [d'un Faune?]." See "L'Apres-Midi d'un Faune" (#7).

[24–25] "[Une Ballade des Femmes Per?]dues." See "Une Ballade des Femmes Perdues" (#10).

[26] "[?] Bathing," burned fragment: 9 lines visible.

[27] "After [Fifty Years?]." See "After Fifty Years" (#4).

[28–30] Untitled, first visible phrase "[?] not on my eyelids." See "Sapphics" (#95).

[31–33] "A Dea[d Dancer?]." See "A Dead Dancer" (#24).

[34] "[?] Storm," burned fragment: parts of 4 lines visible; key visible phrases are "whipping hair," "thin garments to the sun," and "Chicago."

[35] Small drawing of a nude woman

[36] Blank endpaper

165. *The Marble Faun* [*PV:39]

See short title listing *TMF* and *AGB* for publication information. One page of typescript (a) reproduced in *Meriwether:* figure 26. Lines from *TMF* appear in ["Those cries, like scatt[ered silve?]r sails"], #108, which links *TMF* with *TM*. The following 19 poems appear in the published version of *TMF*. (Line counts are given here to provide a comparison with the 1920 typescript line counts listed in entry (a) below.)

PROLOGUE. ["The poplar trees sway to and fro"], 39 lines; pp. 11–12.
I. ["If I were free, then I would go"], 72 lines; pp. 13–15.
II. ["Hark! A sound comes from the brake"], 51 lines; pp. 16–17.
III. ["All the air is gray with rain"], 38 lines; pp. 18–19.
IV. ["The poplars look beyond the wall"], 30 lines, pp. 20–21.
V. ["On the downs beyond the trees"], 50 lines; pp. 22–24.
VI. ["Upon a wood's dim shaded edge"], 74 lines; pp. 25–27.
VII. ["Cawing rooks in tangled flight"], 40 lines; pp. 28–29.
VIII. ["I am sad, nor yet can I"], 55 lines; pp. 30–32.
IX. ["The ringèd moon sits eerily"], 36 lines; pp. 33–34.
X. ["The world is still. How still it is!"], 42 lines; pp. 35–36.
XI. ["The hills are resonant with soft humming"], 44 lines; pp. 37–38.

XII. ["All day I run before a wind"], 38 lines; pp. 39–40.

XIII. ["Now silent autumn fires the trees"], 24 lines; p. 41.

XIV. ["The moon is mad, and dimly burns"], 30 lines; pp. 42–43.

XV. ["The world stands without move or sound"], 32 lines; pp. 44–45.

XVI. ["Why cannot we always be"], 41 lines; pp. 46–47.

XVII. ["Days and nights into years weave"], 42 lines; pp. 48–49.

EPILOGUE. ["May walks in this garden, fair"], 32 lines; dated "April, May June, 1919"; pp. 50–51.

a.   *The Marble Faun.* Unpublished. 27 pp. carbon typescript on legal-size paper; 14 poems bound in soft green paper covers and fastened with grommets at the top; the titles "Prologue," "Spring," "Summer," Noon," "Autumn," "Winter," and "Epilogue" mark the major divisions; minor black ink holograph corrections throughout, probably in Phil Stone's hand; Roman numerals for each poem have been typed onto carbon; three leaves are dated "April, 1920"; this version was considerably revised and rearranged for the 1924 publication and is discussed in Kreisworth 1980, *Origins,* and *Stylization;* TxU. Poems appearing in this version are listed below.

PROLOGUE. ["The poplar trees sway to and fro"], 2 pp. carbon typescript: 39 lines, all complete; holograph revisions probably in Phil Stone's hand; "William Faulkner" typed at bottom of second page.

I. "Spring," 2 pp. carbon typescript: 34 lines, all complete; first line "If I were free, then I would go"; "William Faulkner" typed at bottom of second page.

II. ["Hark! A sound comes from the brake"], 2 pp. carbon typescript: 53 lines, all complete; "William Faulkner" typed at bottom of second page.

III. ["All the air is gray with rain"], 2 pp. carbon typescript: 40 lines, all complete; "William Faulkner / April, 1920" typed at bottom of second page.

IV. ["The hushèd earth, so calm and old"], 1 p. carbon typescript: 26 lines; "William Faulkner" typed at bottom.

V. "Summer," 2 pp. carbon typescript: 36 lines, all complete; first line, "The brook has now become a stream."

VI. "Noon," 3 pp. carbon typescript: 58 lines; first line "Now the blackbirds' gold-wired throats"; "William Faulkner / April, 1920" typed at bottom of third page.

VII. ["The westering sun has climbed the wall"], 2 pp. carbon typescript: 32 lines, all complete; "William Faulkner" typed at bottom of poem.

VIII. ["The world is still. How still it is"], 1 p. carbon typescript: 32 lines, all complete; "William Faulkner." typed at bottom of page.

IX. ["Why cannot we always be"], 2 pp. carbon typescript: 62 lines, all complete; "William Faulkner" at bottom of first page appears to be typed onto carbon; poem continues on second page below a canceled numeral "IX"; final line added in ink, probably in Phil Stone's hand.

X. "Autumn," 2 pp. carbon typescript: 46 lines, all complete; first line "All day I run before the wind"; "William Faulkner" typed at bottom of second page.

XI. ["Cawing rooks in tangled flight"], 2 pp. carbon typescript: 49 lines, all complete; "William Faulkner / April, 1920" typed at bottom of second page.

XII. "Winter," 2 pp. carbon typescript: 42 lines, all complete; first line "The trees stand without move or sound"; "William Faulkner" at bottom of second page has been typed onto carbon.

EPILOGUE. ["May lies in this garden, fair"], 2 pp. carbon typescript 36 lines, all complete; 1 holograph line addition, probably in Phil Stone's hand; "William Faulkner" typed at bottom of second page.

Note: The following typescripts, (b) through (j), contain passages that correspond closely with passages in TMF.

b. Untitled, 19 pp. purple ribbon typescript: burned fragments, few lines complete; several holograph revisions; these leaves appear to belong to a single typescript which corresponds closely with pp. 28 through 49 of the published version; TxU.

c. Untitled, 11 pp. black ribbon typescript: burned fragments; these appear to be part of an early draft, corresponding, but not closely, with pp. 12, 23, 24, 27, 29, 34, 36, and 38 of the published version; TxU.

d. Untitled, 1 p. black ribbon typescript: burned fragment, 28 lines visible, 23 complete; first line "Sunset stains the western sky"; penciled holograph "VI" and "16" above poem; 4 penciled holograph corrections; first 11 lines correspond closely with *TMF,* p. 27; TxU.

e. Untitled, 1 p. black ribbon typescript: burned fragment, 24 lines visible, 20 complete; first visible line "As I lie here my fancy goes"; version of *TMF,* pp. 26–27; TxU.

f. Untitled, 1 p. black ribbon typescript in upper case: burned fragment, 22 lines visible, 20 complete; first visible line "Along a brooding moon wet hill"; lines correspond with *TMF,* pp. 33, 34, and 36 and with 1920 *TMF* IV, lines 7 through 14 and 16 through 18; TxU.

g. Untitled, 1 p. typescript: burned fragment, 19 lines visible, 14 complete; first visible line "Stri[ck?]en by the winds that strum"; one substantive difference from *TMF*, pp. 37–38, lines 6 through 24; TxU.

h. Untitled, 1 p. typescript: burned fragment, 27 lines visible, 26 complete; first visible line "Sending the shatter[ed?] echoes crying"; 2 holograph corrections in Faulkner's 1920 *Marionettes* handwriting; contains phrases that correspond to phrases in *TMF*, pp. 13–14; TxU.

i. Untitled, 1 p. black ribbon typescript: burned fragment, 28 lines visible, 24 complete; first visible line "All day I ran before a wind"; "XVIII" penciled at top; 2 penciled corrections, probably by Phil Stone; corresponds with *TMF*, p. 39; TxU.

j. Untitled, 1 p. black ribbon typescript: burned fragment, 24 lines visible, 19 complete; first complete line "Above me stand the inky trees"; some lines correspond to *TMF* pp. 31-32; *H/B 1982:* 27c. See also Brodsky's published fragments ["Below the misted rainbow falls"] (#12) and ["Her tears are what men call dew"] (#46), which are similar to but do not correspond with lines from *TMF*.

Note: Typescripts (k) through (t), which follow, are similar to but do not correspond with passages in either the published version of TMF *or the 1920 typescript.*

k. Untitled, 1 p. black ribbon typescript: burned fragment, 26 lines visible, 23 complete; first visible phrase "in liquid drops"; TxU.

l. Untitled, 1 p. black ribbon typescript: burned fragment, 25 lines visible, 22 complete; first visible line "The world is still. How still it is"; "XXIV" penciled at top; TxU.

m. Untitled, 1 p. black ribbon typescript: burned fragment, 27 lines visible, 24 complete; first visible phrase "flattering hands"; TxU.

n. Untitled, 1 p. typescript: burned fragment, but all 15 lines, 1 canceled, are complete; first visible line "Above the earth, whose tireless cold"; 1 holograph correction; TxU.

o. Untitled, 1 p. black ribbon typescript: burned fragment, 24 lines visible, 11 complete; first visible line "The running sea [ru?]ns out"; TxU.

p. Untitled, 1 p. black ribbon typescript: burned fragment, 24 lines visible, 10 complete; first visible phrase "A rift of sudden [b?]lue"; "William Faulkner. April 1920." typed at bottom; TxU.

q. Untitled, 1 p. typescript: burned fragment, 24 lines visible, 22 complete; first visible line "Hearkening the pool [?]allaby"; TxU.

r. Untitled, 1 p. typescript: burned fragment, 24 lines visible, 8 complete; second visible phrase "and bound soundlessly"; "William Faulkner" typed at bottom; TxU.

s. Untitled, 1 p. typescript: burned fragment, 28 lines visible, 26 complete; first visible line "Luxuriously until [ni?]ght spills"; TxU.

t. Untitled, 1 p. black ribbon typescript: burned fragment, 21 lines visible, 14 complete; first visible phrase "dreamed it, saving they"; TxU.

u. A series of burned fragments with few if any lines complete appear to contain versions of lines from *TMF,* but because they are in such fragmentary condition, they are not catalogued individually here; TxU.

166. *Michael Sequence Fragments* (listed elsewhere as *Michael*)

Unpublished. *Michael* is the title of a long, undated poem or poem sequence, consisting of at least 40 sections. Only assorted fragments of *Michael* survived the Stone fire; of these remnants, 9 leaves belong to the Wynn Collection. Other burned fragments in the Wynn, Brodsky, and TxU Collections bear stylistic and thematic similarities (see *[Texas]*, #169), but I list here only the Wynn leaves because 7 of them mention Michael by name and the other 2 appear to be continuations of the poems on these leaves. In some cases the leaves are probably consecutive but not certainly so; therefore, one cannot be sure that the fragments include the whole of any of these poems as they appeared in *Michael.* For this reason, I have separated the physical description of the leaves from the description of the poems. Thus, readers can compare the descriptions of the scattered leaves (A through I below) with the descriptions of the poems (a through i). Only one *Michael* poem has been published (a); other manuscripts and publications of this poem may be found in the published listings. Other *Michael* poems appear only in this entry. MsU (Wynn, folder 1, #1–9).

Leaf A: typescript: burned fragment, 23 lines visible, 20 complete.

Leaf B: typescript: burned fragment, 26 lines visible, 21 complete.

Leaf C: typescript: burned fragment, bottom of page cut, 21 lines visible and complete.

Leaf D: typescript: burned fragment, page cut at top, 16 lines visible, 15 complete.

Leaf E: typescript: burned fragment, page cut at top, 20 lines visible, 17 complete.

Leaf F: typescript: burned fragment, 6 quatrains visible, all but last quatrain complete.

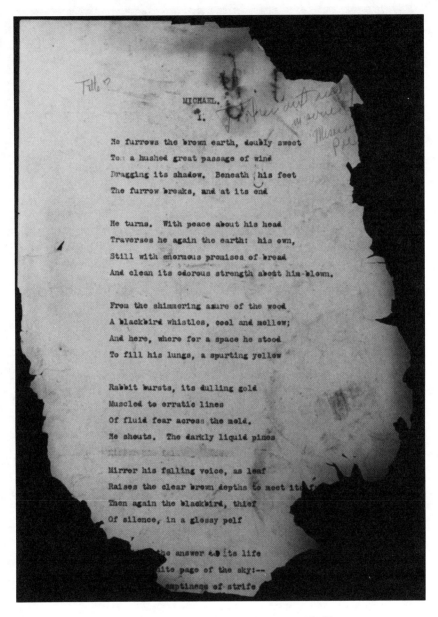

Figure 35. Leaf A from *Michael* Sequence Fragment (#166)
(Courtesy Jill Faulkner Summers and the University of Mississippi Library)

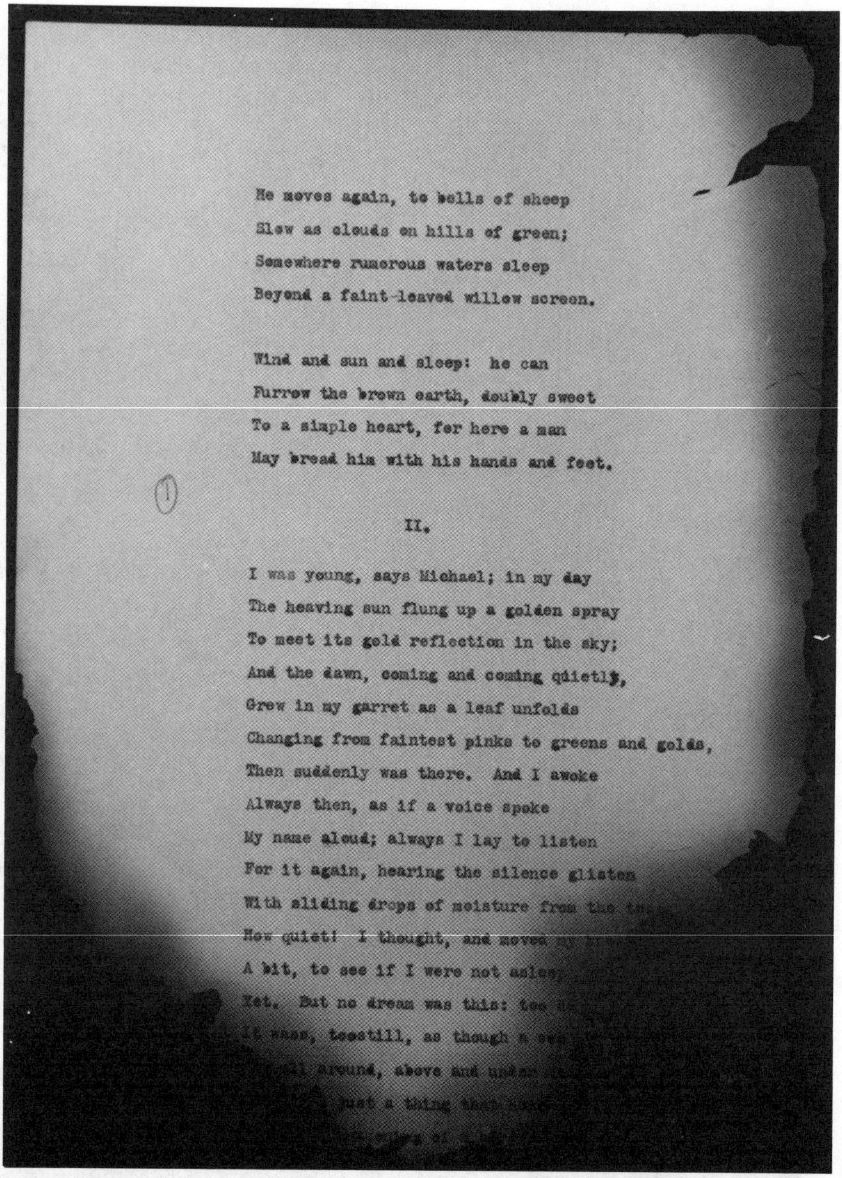

He moves again, to bells of sheep
Slow as clouds on hills of green;
Somewhere rumorous waters sleep
Beyond a faint-leaved willow screen.

Wind and sun and sleep: he can
Furrow the brown earth, doubly sweet
To a simple heart, for here a man
May bread him with his hands and feet.

II.

I was young, says Michael; in my day
The heaving sun flung up a golden spray
To meet its gold reflection in the sky;
And the dawn, coming and coming quietly,
Grew in my garret as a leaf unfolds
Changing from faintest pinks to greens and golds,
Then suddenly was there. And I awoke
Always then, as if a voice spoke
My name aloud; always I lay to listen
For it again, hearing the silence glisten
With sliding drops of moisture from the tr
How quiet! I thought, and moved my h
A bit, to see if I were not aslee
Yet. But no dream was this: too s
It wass, toostill, as though a sea
Around, above and under
just a thing that

Figure 36.   Leaf B from *Michael* Sequence Fragment (#166)
(*Courtesy Jill Faulkner Summers and the University of
Mississippi Library*)

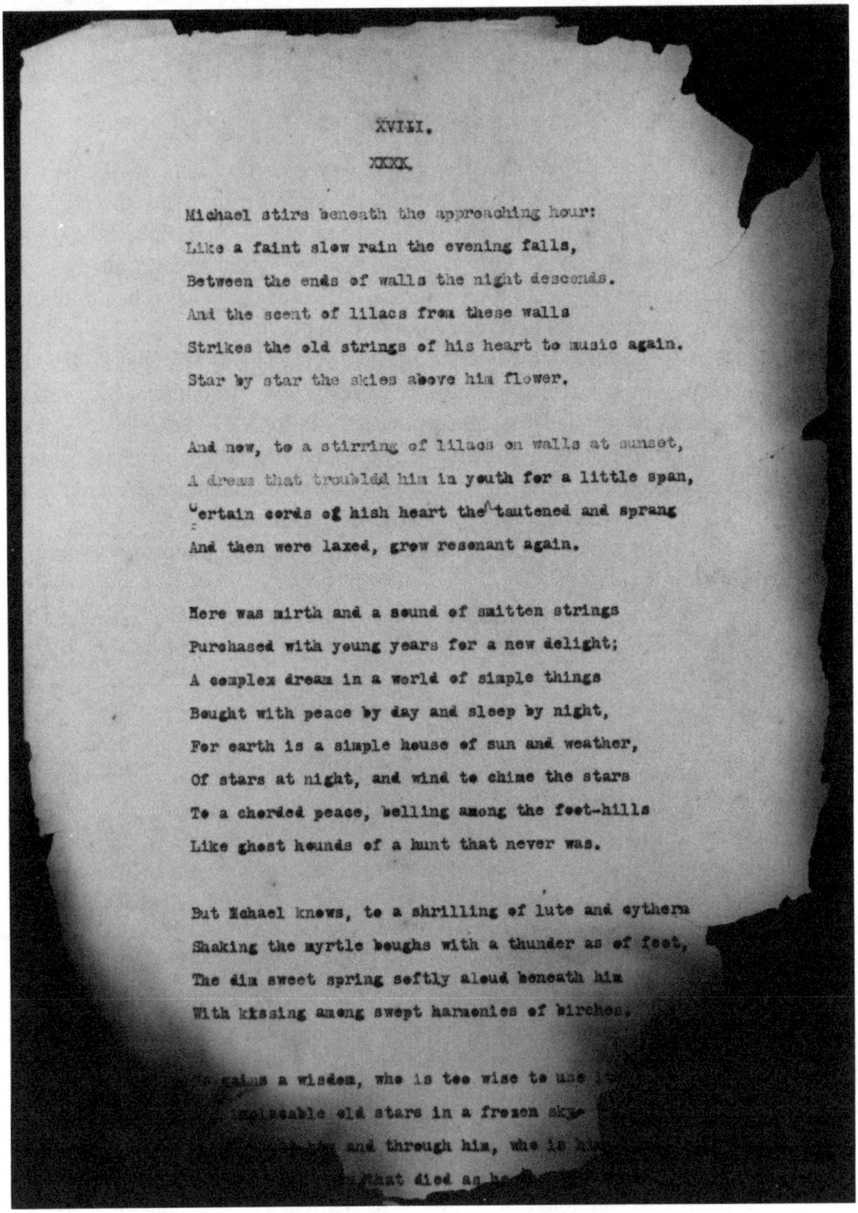

XVIII.

XXXX.

Michael stirs beneath the approaching hour:
Like a faint slow rain the evening falls,
Between the ends of walls the night descends.
And the scent of lilacs from these walls
Strikes the old strings of his heart to music again.
Star by star the skies above him flower.

And now, to a stirring of lilacs on walls at sunset,
A dream that troubled him in youth for a little span,
Certain cords of hish heart the tautened and sprang
And then were laxed, grow resonant again.

Here was mirth and a sound of smitten strings
Purchased with young years for a new delight;
A complex dream in a world of simple things
Bought with peace by day and sleep by night,
For earth is a simple house of sun and weather,
Of stars at night, and wind to chime the stars
To a chorded peace, belling among the foot-hills
Like ghost hounds of a hunt that never was.

But Michael knows, to a shrilling of lute and cythern
Shaking the myrtle boughs with a thunder as of feet,
The dim sweet spring softly aloud beneath him
With kissing among swept harmonies of birches.

. . . . gains a wisdom, who is too wise to use . . .
. . . . immiscable old stars in a frozen sky . . .
. . . . and through him, who is hi. . .
. . . . that died as h. . .

Figure 37. Leaf I from *Michael* Sequence Fragment (#166)
*(Courtesy Jill Faulkner Summers and the University of
Mississippi Library)*

Leaf G: typescript: burned fragment, bottom of page cut off, 2 quatrains visible and complete.

Leaf H: typescript: burned fragment, bottom of page cut, 4 lines visible and complete.

Leaf I: typescript: burned fragment, 26 lines visible, 23 complete.

a. ["He furrows the brown earth, doubly sweet"]. This is *Michael* I, comprising 6 quatrains on leaf A and 2 quatrains on leaf B; "Michael / (Roman numeral) I." typed above first line; holograph Arabic numeral "1" circled in left margin below second quatrain of leaf B and above Roman numeral "II"; see #43 for other publications, typescripts, and manuscripts.

b. ["I was young, says Michael; in my day"]. This is *Michael* II, beginning with last 18 lines of leaf B and possibly continuing with similar stanzas of rhymed couplets on leaf C.

c. ["That here passed something it and I"]. Although Michael is not mentioned by name, this is apparently a fragment of *Michael* and possibly a continuation of *Michael* II; constitutes leaf C.

d. ["Michael lifts his ruined face to starlight"]. 4 quatrains constituting leaf D.

e. ["The hour comes on gusts of faint confetti"]. Although Michael is not mentioned by name, this is apparently a fragment of *Michael* and possibly part of XVII (see (f) below); constitutes leaf E.

f. ["And Michael hears, superbly quiet in his window"]. Last 3 quatrains of *Michael* XVIII; constitutes 3 quatrains of leaf F; penciled in left margin are the notations "3," "2," and "you mean 12," notations that may refer to *Michael* XIX, which follows.

g. ["A carnival flares: the world beneath him is passing"]. This is the beginning of *Michael* XIX; constitutes last 3 quatrains of leaf F, and concludes with the 2 stanzas on leaf G that precede "XX" typed above cut at bottom of page.

h. ["Then he and I together, without thought, regarding"]. Constitutes leaf H; since "XXIV" is typed at bottom, above cut, this is *Michael* XXIII; holograph "3" and "3" circled in left margin.

i. ["Michael stirs beneath the approaching hour"]. This is *Michael* "XXXX" [*sic*] ("XVIII" canceled above "XXXX"); constitutes leaf I.

167. *Mississippi Poems*

For published versions, see short-title listings *HC/MP* and *MP 1979*. Reproduction of title page of typescript (a) appears in *H/B 1982:* 37 (figure 14).

a. *Mississippi Poems*, 12 pp. carbon typescript with typed cover sheet; "Oxford, Mississippi, / October, 1924" and "William Faulkner" typed on cover; "Autographed for Myrtle Ramey / 30 day of December, 1924 / William Faulkner" added in holograph; on each page, including cover, is written, probably by Phil Stone, "Publication rights reserved. Not to be published without the written consent of the author or Phil Stone"; first 7 poems numbered, last 5 unnumbered; 9 titled; *H/B 1982:* 45. Manuscript includes the following poems (see individual entries for other publications, typescripts, and manuscripts).

I. ["Shall I recall this tree, when I am old"]. See #96.
II. ["Moon of death, moon of bright despair"]. See #71.
III. "Indian Summer." See #54.
IV. "Wild Geese." See #121.
V. ["He furrows the brown earth, doubly sweet"]. See #43.
VI. "The Poet Goes Blind." See #84.
VII. "Mississippi Hills: My Epitaph." See #70.
[i.] "March." See #67.
[ii.] "The Gallows." See #38.
[iii.] "Pregnacy." See #87.
[iv.] "November 11th." See #75.
[v.] "December: / To Elise." See #26.

b. *Mississippi Poems*. Unpublished. 11 pp. ribbon typescript with 7 poems sequenced by Roman numeral and 2 unnumbered poems. Title page in holograph, with "Oxford, Mississippi / October, 1924" and "William Faulkner" at bottom; the notation "all this in caps" appears beside title; other notations and changes in accidentals (in all poem titles and in poems II, III, VI and "November 11th") indicate that the Wynn version was the copy from which carbon typescript (a) was typed; six substantive holograph corrections; includes same poems as carbon typescript (a) above, but excludes 3 unnumbered poems ("March," "December: / To Elise" and "Pregnacy"; "November 11th" in this typescript includes a dedication, "In memory of B——, Royal Air Force," which does not appear in typescript (a); MsU (Wynn, folder 7, folder 6, #31, and folder 5, #30).

168. [*University of Mississippi Housman Sequence Fragments*] (listed elsewhere as [*Housman*])

Unpublished. 4 leaves in the Wynn Collection appear to be fragments of a long poem sequence of Housman-like lyrics. As in the case of

[*Michael*], the leaves are assorted fragments: the first 2 leaves (A and B), with Roman numerals "V." and "VI." typed midpage on each leaf, and the last 2 (C through D), with Roman numerals "XI." and "XII." typed midpage, may be consecutive, but are not certainly so; the leaves often contain more than 1 poem, and one cannot always be sure that a leaf contains the complete poem. For these reasons, the physical description of the leaves (A through D) will be followed by a description of the 6 individual extant poems in the sequence (a through d); MsU (Wynn, folder 2, #10–13).

Leaf A: typescript: burned fragment, 3 quatrains plus 4 lines (quatrain?) visible; all but last line complete; the last 4 lines are untitled but preceded by "V."

Leaf B: typescript: burned fragment, 6 quatrains visible and complete; first 2 quatrains appear to conclude "V." on leaf A; last 4 quatrains are untitled but preceded by "VI."

Leaf C: typescript: burned fragment, 4 quatrains visible and complete; top of page cut.

Leaf D: typescript: burned fragment, 5 quatrains plus 4 lines (quatrain?) visible, all complete except last 4 lines; "XII." following first 2 quatrains.

a. ["When I rose up with morning"], first 3 quatrains of leaf A, if complete; "3" is circled in left margin with penciled remark, "Too much Shropshire Lad"; this is [*Housman*] IV; for published version (which has one substantive variant) and other manuscripts of this poem, see #118.

b. ["Never is living quiet"], last, incomplete stanza on leaf A and probably first 2 quatrains on leaf B; penciled in left margin of leaf B after second quatrain are "3," "3," and "perhaps 4"; this is [*Housman*] V; for other typescript, see #139.

c. ["Turn again, Dick Whittington"], last 4 quatrains on leaf B; this is [*Housman*] VI; for published version (which has slight substantive variants) and other manuscripts, see #112.

d. ["I give the world to love you"], first 3 quatrains of leaf C, if complete; "3" and "3" are circled in left margin with penciled remark, "Poor Shropshire Lad"; this is [*Housman*] X; for published versions and other manuscripts, see #50.

e. ["O Thyrsis, he's the lover"], fourth quatrain on leaf C and first 2 quatrains on leaf D; "3" and "3" circled in margin of leaf D at end of poem; this is [*Housman*] XI; this poem exists only in this manuscript.

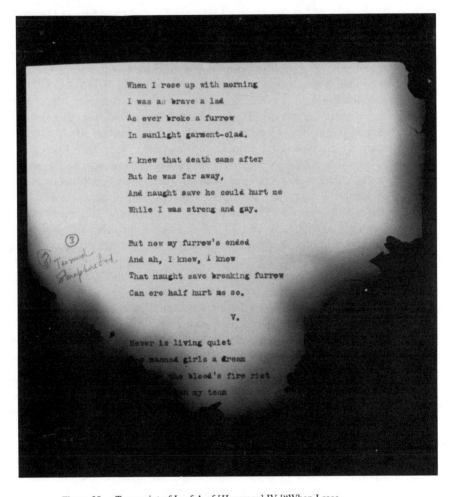

Figure 38. Typescript of Leaf A of [*Housman*] IV ["When I rose
up with morning"] (#168)
This poem appears again in another grouping of poems (#160).
*(Courtesy Jill Faulkner Summers and the University of
Mississippi Library)*

f.   ["Diana, put by your bow and spear"], last 3 quatrains and 3 incomplete lines of fourth quatrain on leaf D; Roman numeral "XII." typed above poem; this is [*Housman*] XII; see #131 for other manuscripts.

169. [*University of Texas Sequence Fragments*] (listed elsewhere as [*Texas*])

Unpublished. 35 pp. purple ribbon typescript: burned fragments which are tonally and thematically similar to *VIS* and *Michael* but do not correspond with any specific poem in any identified sequence or sequence fragment. These leaves may contain early versions of *VIS*, *Michael*, the now lost *Orpheus* sequence, or another unknown sequence or long poem dating from this period. Typographical evidence indicates that these 28 burned fragments as well as 7 burned fragments in the Brodsky collection† are all leaves of 1 sequence or long poem: they are all typed with purple ribbon; Roman numerals are interspersed throughout the leaves, and penciled on the other sides of all but 4 leaves are holograph fragments of another long poem. 2 of these 4 leaves contain penciled holograph drafts of Faulkner's 1921 review of Conrad Aiken's *Turns and Movies* (see *Origins:* 105–25), and 2 have nothing on the other side. Often the holograph fragments repeat lines and phrases from the typescripts; 4 of these holograph fragments contain passages corresponding with *VIS* IX, "Love Song" (see #64). Butterworth catalogues the [*Texas*] fragments at TxU as the [Prufrock Poem] [*UV:28a]; Brodsky calls his leaves the "Stone Fragments"; here I list them individually as leaves A through II, providing first visible lines or phrases of typescripts and holographs. These leaves are listed alphabetically by first visible phrase of the typescript.

Leaf A: ["and settles down [to?] sleep"]. First visible phrase of 1 p. purple ribbon typescript: burned fragment; other side is blank; TxU.

Leaf B: ["as morning dawned"]. First visible phrase of 1 p. purple ribbon typescript: burned fragment; on other side is penciled holograph fragment beginning "dust in empty rooms"; TxU.

Leaf C: ["ask them all, I will stop them as"]. First visible phrase of 1 p. purple ribbon typescript: burned fragment; "XII" appears on leaf; on other side is penciled holograph beginning "and greenly flame to the sun's slow lidless blaze"; TxU.

Leaf D: ["before me, and lay down"]. First visible phrase of 1 p. purple ribbon typescript: burned fragment; "LXIV" appears on leaf; on other

---

†Photocopies of the typescript sides of *H/B 1982:* 27d-j and Brodsky's catalogue descriptions provide evidence for including these leaves here.

side is penciled holograph fragment beginning "Leads to naught?";
TxU.

Leaf E: ["brittle boughs upon the tortured"]. First visible phrase of 1 p.
purple ribbon typescript; penciled holograph fragment beginning
"[tu?]rning endless pages" on other side (see "Love Song," #64d);
TxU.

Leaf F: ["[b?]uilt ourselves / [?] and cannot cry"]. Ends of first two visible lines of 1 p. purple ribbon typescript: burned fragment; on other
side is penciled holograph fragment beginning "me alone"; TxU.

Leaf G: ["crowds against his legs"]. First visible phrase of 1 p. purple
ribbon typescript: burned fragment; "IX" appears on page; on other
side is penciled holograph fragment beginning "the waves upon him
whitely blown"; TxU.

Leaf H: ["the earth grows dark"]. First visible phrase of 1 p. purple
ribbon typescript: burned fragment; on other side is penciled holograph
fragment beginning "that night has come" (see "Love Song," #64b);
TxU.

Leaf I: ["the forms he dreamed"]. First visible phrase of 1 p. purple
ribbon typescript: burned fragment, parts of 26 lines visible; Roman
numeral "III" above last 5 lines; on other side is penciled holograph
fragment of "Love Song." First visible line "Does not each fold" (see
#64f); TxU.

Leaf J: ["fruits of bright desire"]. First visible phrase of 1 p. purple ribbon
typescript: burned fragment; on other side is penciled holograph fragment beginning "[team?]ing brain" (see "Love Song," #64e); TxU.

Leaf K: ["in a caverned brain"]. First visible phrase of 1 p. purple ribbon
typescript: burned fragment, parts of 21 lines visible; on other side is
14-line penciled holograph fragment beginning "the dark whence all
are born"; *H/B 1982:* 27e.

Leaf L: ["in floorless halls"]. First visible phrase of 1 p. purple ribbon
typescript: burned fragment; "(end)" typed at bottom; on other side is
penciled holograph fragment beginning "And the gleam of the
dark[ening?]"; TxU.

Leaf M: ["in your slim hands"]. First visible phrase of 1 p. purple ribbon
typescript: burned fragment, parts of 24 lines visible; on other side is
penciled holograph manuscript which has been reproduced and is listed
separately by its first visible phrase "last beauty" (#58a); *H/B 1982:*
27h.

Leaf N: ["it matters not which one"]. First visible phrase of 1 p. purple
ribbon typescript which has been reproduced and is listed separately
above (see #56): burned fragment, 25 lines visible, 11 complete; on

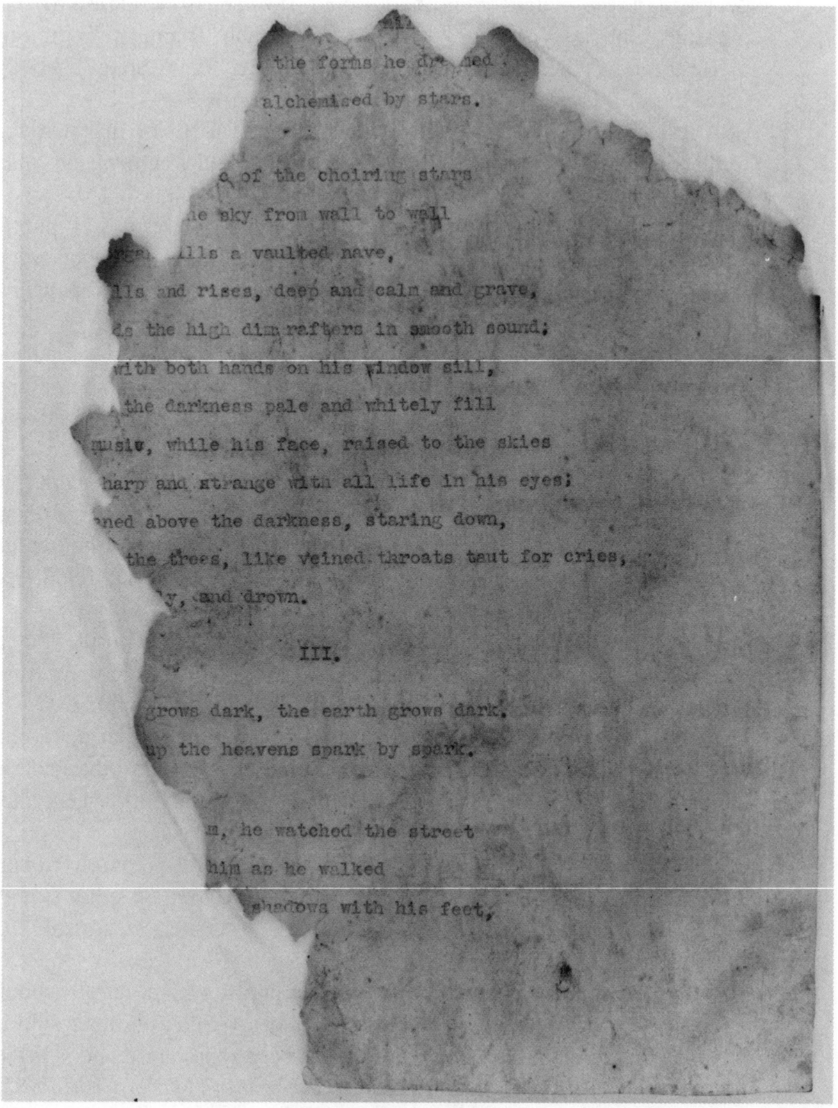

the forms he dr...ned
alchemised by stars.

...of the choiring stars
...e sky from wall to wall
...lls a vaulted nave,
...ls and rises, deep and calm and grave,
...s the high dim rafters in smooth sound;
with both hands on his window sill,
...the darkness pale and whitely fill
...usic, while his face, raised to the skies
...harp and strange with all life in his eyes;
...ned above the darkness, staring down,
...the trees, like veined throats taut for cries,
...y, and drown.

III.

...grows dark, the earth grows dark.
...p the heavens spark by spark.

...m, he watched the street
...him as he walked
...shadows with his feet,

Figure 39. Typescript Side of [*Texas*], Leaf I (#169)
(*Courtesy Jill Faulkner Summers and the Harry Ransom
Humanities Research Center, The University of Texas, Austin*)

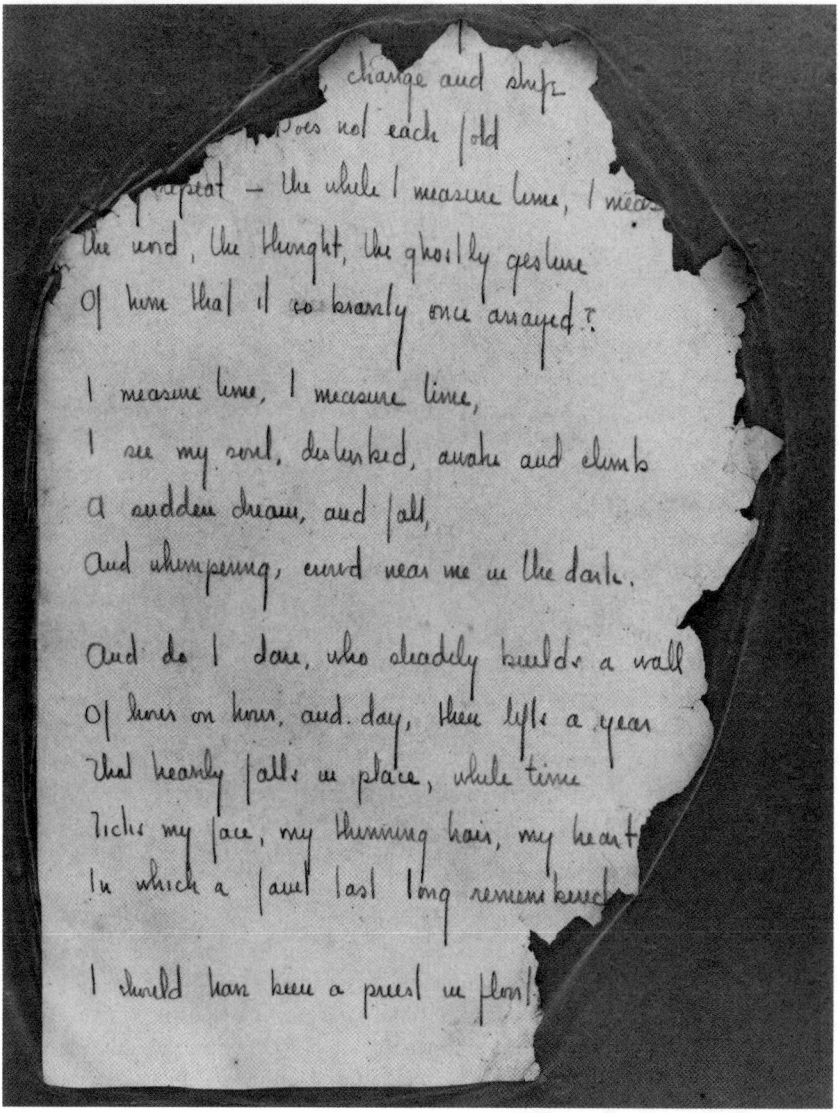

Figure 40. Manuscript Side of [*Texas*], Leaf I (#169)
(*Courtesy Jill Faulkner Summers and the Harry Ransom
Humanities Research Center, The University of Texas, Austin*)

other side is penciled holograph version of Faulkner's Aiken review beginning "impersonality will never permit him to"; TxU.

Leaf O: ["of sound"]. First of 2 lines on 1 p. purple ribbon typescript: burned fragment; on other side is penciled holograph fragment beginning "small hand"; TxU.

Leaf P: ["prisoned self and rise"]. First visible phrase of 1 p. purple ribbon typescript: burned fragment; on other side is penciled holograph fragment beginning "alone. I will walk alone" (see "Love Song," #64c); TxU.

Leaf Q: ["[Remem?]ber that first strange passionate spring"]. Fourth line of 1 p. purple ribbon typescript: burned fragment, parts of 21 lines visible; on other side is penciled holograph fragment beginning "let us talk of those dark silent days"; *H/B 1982:* 27i.

Leaf R: ["rose and leaned its breast upon the horizon"]. First visible line of 1 p. purple ribbon typescript: burned fragment, parts of 18 lines visible; on other side is penciled holograph fragment beginning "It was you who, in a certain dark"; *H/B 1982:* 27d.

Leaf S: ["the same, always the same"]. First visible phrase of 1 p. purple ribbon typescript: burned fragment, parts of 15 lines complete; on other side is 14-line penciled holograph fragment beginning "Do you remember that ['strange' (*del.*)] first strange passionate spring"; *H/B 1982:* 27j.

Leaf T: ["slowly miring in futility"]. First visible phrase of 1 p. purple ribbon typescript: burned fragment; "XI" on page; on other side is penciled holograph fragment beginning "And there is so little here in this"; TxU.

Leaf U: ["space into a violin"]. First visible phrase of 1 p. purple ribbon typescript which has been reproduced and is listed separately above (see #58b): burned fragment, parts of 23 lines visible; on other side is penciled holograph fragment with the tenth line "down past the somber hills"; *H/B 1982:* 27g.

Leaf V: ["swing wet boughs across his face"]. First visible phrase of 1 p. purple ribbon typescript: burned fragment; on other side is penciled holograph fragment beginning "to seek and cry in [?]"; TxU.

Leaf W: ["thinking, I"]. First visible phrase of 1 p. purple ribbon typescript: burned fragment, 17 lines visible, 13 complete; on other side is penciled holograph fragment beginning "Now when life lays hands on troubled breasts"; TxU.

Leaf X: ["[th?]is life you bear like an invulnerable shi[eld?]"]. First visible phrase of 1 p. purple ribbon typescript: burned fragment; on other side is penciled holograph fragment beginning "Here a grave stone glimmers in the gloom"; TxU.

Leaf Y: ["this, this thing to me"]. First visible phrase of 1 p. purple ribbon typescript: burned fragment; on other side is penciled holograph fragment beginning "swing wet boughs across his face"; TxU.

Leaf Z: ["throats swell and fill with song"]. First visible phrase of 1 p. purple ribbon typescript: burned fragment; "VI." follows first 4 lines; on other side is penciled holograph fragment "music, played again"; TxU.

Leaf AA: ["to dust? Should we then, li[ke?]"]. First visible line of 1 p. purple ribbon typescript which has been reproduced (see #110): burned fragment, 22 lines visible, 15 complete; on other side is penciled holograph draft of Faulkner's Aiken review beginning "In the fog of generic puberty raised by contemp[orary?] ve[rsifiers?]"; TxU.

Leaf BB: ["to life again through death"]. First visible phrase of 1 p. purple ribbon typescript: burned fragment; on other side is penciled holograph fragment beginning "[wo?]man's dark devastated hair"; TxU.

Leaf CC: ["the trees smooth sunset from the sky"]. First visible phrase of 1 p. purple ribbon typescript: burned fragment; "LXIII." on page; on other side is penciled holograph fragment beginning "Was her singular in the dancers cries"; TxU.

Leaf DD: ["waves upon him whitel[y?] blown"]. First visible phrase of 1 p. purple ribbon typescript: burned fragment, parts of 22 lines visible; on other side is penciled holograph fragment "the forms he dreamed"; TxU.

Leaf EE: ["the western window, sea, the sky"]. First visible phrase of 1 p. purple ribbon typescript: burned fragment; on other side is penciled holograph fragment beginning "and standing so far away"; TxU.

Leaf FF: ["Wet slate roofs turned violet with ra[in?]"]. First visible phrase of 1 p. purple ribbon typescript: burned fragment; on other side is penciled holograph fragment beginning "gold that gleams"; TxU.

Leaf GG: ["Where, then, shall I look? he ponders"]. First visible line of 1 p. purple ribbon typescript: burned fragment; on other side is penciled holograph fragment beginning "I will accost him at this turn"; TxU.

Leaf HH: ["window, senselessly staring down"]. First line of 1 p. purple ribbon typescript: burned fragment; below last line is "XX."; on other side is 15-line penciled holograph fragment beginning "We hear an untouched music pause and sing"; *H/B 1982:* 27f.

Leaf II: ["would run again"]. First visible phrase of 1 p. purple ribbon typescript: burned fragment; other side is blank; TxU.

170. [*University of Virginia Sequence Fragment 1*] (listed elsewhere as [*Virginia 1*])

Unpublished. 9 pp. purple ribbon typescript on legal-size sheets: a broken series of 6 poems. Pagination (partially erased) is typed in parentheses at bottom of each extant leaf. Holograph ink Arabic numerals have been placed above the titles of 4 of the poems. Leaves appear to have once been pinned and stapled or tied together as all have uniform pin marks and cuts or staple marks on both upper corners. "William Faulkner" is typed on lower left sides of all leaves. Sequence fragment includes the following poems, all of which have been published (see individual entries for publications, other typescripts, and manuscripts); ViU.

1. "The Dancer," p. 4. See #21.
2. ["Man comes, man goes; and leaves behind"], p. 1. See #66.
6. "Puck and Death," p. 7. See #89.
8. "Marriage," pp. 9–12. See #69.
[?] "Eunice," pp. 17–19. See #33.
[?] "Philosophy," pp. 21–22. See #82.

171. [*University of Virginia Sequence Fragment 2*] (listed elsewhere as [*Virginia 2*])

Unpublished. 8 pp. black ribbon typescript on legal-size paper. Some poems have penciled but erased titles, not in William Faulkner's hand, and all poems have an Arabic numeral typed above first line. Sequence fragment includes the following poems, all of which have been published (see individual entries for publications, other typescripts, and manuscripts); ViU.

1. ["I will not weep for youth"]. See #53.
2. ["The flowers that died"]. See #36.
3. ["Winter is gone, snow but an old wives tale"]. See #122.
4. ["The sun lay long upon the hills"]. See #106.
5. ["Beyond the hill the sun swam downward"]. See "Twilight," #113.
6. ["Young Richard, striding toward town"]. See #125.
7. ["When evening shadows grew around"]. See #117.
8. ["When I was young and proud and gay"]. See #119.

172. [*University of Virginia Sequence Fragment 3*] (listed elsewhere as [*Virginia 3*])

Unpublished. 7 pp. black ribbon typescript on legal-size paper; a broken series of 5 poems. 3 poems have Arabic numerals added in ink above title

or first line. In upper left corner of each leaf are identically placed
pinholes indicating where poems were originally held together. Sequence
fragment includes the following poems. With the exception of "The Shepherd's Love," all have been published (see individual entries for publications, other typescripts, and manuscripts); ViU.

1. ["Trumpets of sun in silence fall"]. See "Night Piece," #74.
2. "Vision in Spring." See #116.
9. "April." See #8.
[?] "To Elise." See "December: / To Elise," #26.
[?] "The Shepherd's Love." See #151.

173. *Vision in Spring*

For published edition, see short-title listing, *VIS*. For poem "Vision in
Spring," see #116.

a. *Vision in Spring*, 92 pp. photocopy of bound typescript and its holograph hand-printed, hand-painted cover. Original given to Estelle
Oldham Franklin, summer 1921. 88-page poem sequence of 14 poems numbered by Roman numeral in the table of contents; the original of this photocopy is described in *Blotner 1974:* 307–12 and in
VIS introduction (ix–xi) and appendix A (xxxiii–xxxvii); location of
original booklet is unknown; contents of photocopied booklet are
listed below; for other manuscripts, typescripts, and publications of
these poems, see individual entries within this bibliography; original
photocopy JFS; copy available at ViU (Accession #9817-I).

The following 4 pp. of the photocopy are unnumbered:
[1] Cover
[2] Title page reading "VISION IN SPRING / by / W. Faulkner"; at
bottom, "Manuscript Edition. 1921"
[3] Contents page
[4] Blank end page with Faulkner's holograph note in india ink on
rebinding

The following 88 pp. are numbered by Faulkner:
I. "Vision in Spring," pp. 1–5. See #116.
II. "Interlude," pp. 6–9. See #55.
III. "The World and Pierrot. A Nocturne," pp. 10–29. See #123.
IV. "After the Concert," pp. 30–32. See #3.
V. "Portrait," pp. 33–35. See #86.
VI. Untitled, pp. 36–39. See ["The dark ascends"] (#22).
VII. Untitled, pp. 40–46. See "A Symphony" (#107).

VIII. Untitled, pp. 47–54. See ["Rain, rain . . . a field of silver grain"] (#91).

IX. "Love Song," pp. 55–64. See #64.

X. "The Dancer," pp. 65–66. See #21.

XI. Untitled, pp. 67–75. See "Marriage" (#69).

XII. "Orpheus," pp. 76–82. See #80.

XIII. "Philosophy," pp. 83–85. See #82.

XIV. "April," pp 86–88. See #8.

b. *Vision in Spring:* an extended work for soprano and strings. Lyrics from 4 poems in this sequence, "Vision in Spring," "The Dancer," "Orpheus," and "April" were set to music by Jerald Kirk Hughes. Lyrics are printed in the *Program for Symphony North of Houston,* 11 May 1985; NN-B, ViU.

4

Poem Fragments

174. ["Aelia, at the casement of despair"] [*UF:1]

    First complete (fifth) phrase of 1 p. typescript: burned fragment, 13 lines visible, 10 complete; TxU.

175. ["And can the woven fabric's sorry fold"] [*UF:6]

    First complete (fourth) line of 1 p. typescript: burned fragment, 12 lines visible, all but first 3 complete; TxU.

176. ["And nymph and satyr follow Pan"] [*UF:7]

    First line of fragments below.

    a. Untitled, 1 p. purple carbon typescript: burned fragment, 24 lines visible, 17 complete; TxU.
    b. Untitled, 1 p. carbon typescript: burned fragment, 17 lines visible, 13 complete; TxU.

177. ["And then we'll both forget our sorrow"]

    First visible phrase of 1 p. black ribbon typescript: burned fragment, 15 lines visible, 11 complete; TxU.

178. ["birth / earth"] [*UF:10]

    Line-ends of 1 p. typescript: burned fragment, parts of 2 lines visible; "William Faulkner" typed at bottom; TxU.

179. ["By this white body shortening into mine"] [*UF:15]

    First line 1 p. carbon typescript: burned fragment, 4 quatrains visible, 12 lines complete; TxU.

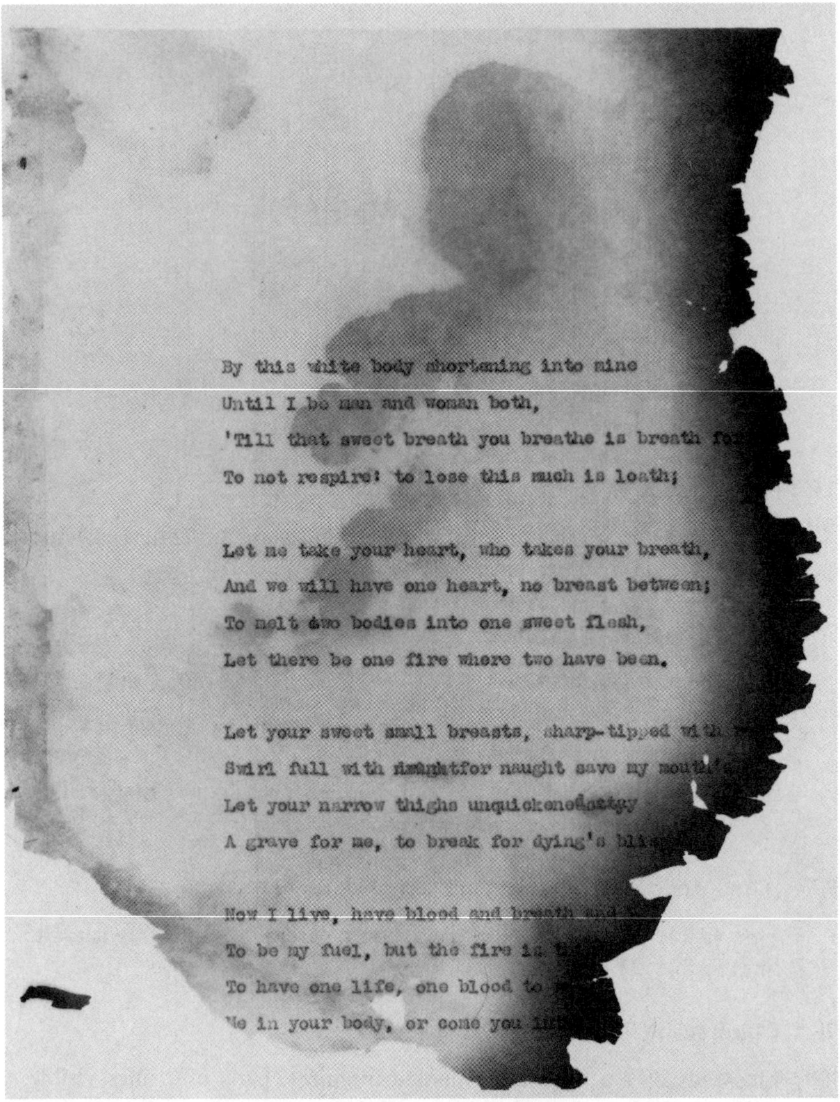

By this white body shortening into mine
Until I be man and woman both,
'Till that sweet breath you breathe is breath fo...
To not respire: to lose this much is loath;

Let me take your heart, who takes your breath,
And we will have one heart, no breast between;
To melt two bodies into one sweet flesh,
Let there be one fire where two have been.

Let your sweet small breasts, sharp-tipped with ...
Swirl full with ...tfor naught save my mouth...
Let your narrow thighs unquickened...
A grave for me, to break for dying's bli...

Now I live, have blood and breath and ...
To be my fuel, but the fire is ...
To have one life, one blood to ...
Me in your body, or come you ...

Figure 41.   Unidentified, Burned Poem Fragment ["By this white
body shortening into mine"] (#179)
*(Courtesy Jill Faulkner Summers and the Harry Ransom
Humanities Research Center, The University of Texas, Austin)*

180. ["Concealed pool where she bathed [?] saw her bare"] [*UF:16]

Second visible line 1 p. typescript: burned fragment, 5 quatrains visible, all but last 2 lines complete; TxU.

181. ["fill the skies"]

First visible phrase of 1 p. typescript: burned fragment, 7 lines visible, 4 complete; appears to be an incomplete sonnet; TxU.

182. ["flowers / bloom / hours / [?] overs / [?] / covers"] [*UF:20]

Line-ends of 1 p. typescript: burned fragment, parts of 13 lines visible; TxU.

183. ["For a maid may smile and call you true"] [*UF:21]

First line last stanza 1 p. purple ribbon typescript: burned fragment, 8 lines visible, 4 complete; TxU.

184. ["Forgotten his pints"] [*UF:22]

First line of 1 p. penciled manuscript: burned fragment, 2 lines visible; this is on other side of 1 p. manuscript listed separately as ["glad, how peaceful! and an answering echo within him"] (#186); TxU.

185. ["From the swept dunes, to the sky"]

First line of the following fragments.

a. 1 p. purple ribbon typescript: burned fragment, 24 lines visible, 14 complete; "XXV." at top of poem; TxU.
b. 1 p. black ribbon typescript: burned fragment, 20 lines visible, 13 complete; TxU.

186. ["glad, how peaceful! and an answering echo within him"] [*UF:24]

First visible line of 1 p. penciled manuscript: burned fragment, 19 lines, 4 canceled; on other side is 1 p. manuscript listed separately as ["Forgotten his pints"] (#184); TxU.

187. ["the grasses to a sound"]

First visible phrase of 1 p. black ribbon typescript: burned fragment, parts of 14 lines visible; 2 corrections not in Faulkner's hand; TxU.

188.   ["[?] he gaped and cried"]

Incomplete first line of 1 p. ink holograph manuscript: burned fragment, 44 lines visible, only last 6 lines complete; 3 lines canceled; on other side are three holograph drafts of "The Gallows" (see #38i); MsU (Wynn, folder 9).

189.   ["Let lisp of leaves and drowsy birds"] [*UF:30]

First line of fragments below.

   a.   Untitled, 1 p. purple ribbon typescript: burned fragment, 24 lines visible, 16 complete; TxU.
   b.   Untitled, 1 p. carbon typescript: burned fragment, 24 lines visible, 14 complete; 1 holograph correction; (b) completes burned lines (except last line) in (a) above; TxU.

190.   ["let's buy us ple[asu?]re"] [*UF:53]

First visible phrase of 1 p. black ribbon typescript: burned fragment, 3 quatrains visible, 7 lines complete; TxU.

191.   ["The meadow, the shadowy water"]

Photocopy of holograph manuscript: burned fragment, 18 lines; given to Bell I. Wiley by Phil Stone, ca. 1941 (see *Bonner:* 150); LNT.

192.   "Music dying languidly in darkness"

Title of 1 p. ink holograph manuscript: 4-line fragment; first line "The darkness shakes its hair"; ViU (Accession #9817-b).

193.   ["O Pan! who binds with fear both beast and clod"] [*UF:37]

First complete line 1 p. purple ribbon typescript: burned fragment, 9 lines visible, 6 complete; "William Faulkner" typed at bottom; TxU.

194.   ["Of another day [?]"]

First visible phrase of 1 p. black ribbon typescript: burned fragment, parts of 14 lines visible; black ink "p" and arrows in right margin; TxU.

195. ["Of starlit stream and frostbound clod"] [*UF:38]

    First line of fragments below.

    a. Untitled, 1 p. purple ribbon typescript: burned fragment, 24 lines visible, 16 complete; TxU.
    b. Untitled, 1 p. carbon typescript: burned fragment, 24 lines visible, 19 complete; this is not a carbon of (a) above; TxU.

196. ["the quick stream's me[lte?]d snow"]

    First visible phrase of 1 p. black ribbon typescript: burned fragment, 9 lines visible, 6 complete; "William Faulkner." typed at bottom; TxU.

197. ["Reft me of brain, begot on me"] [*UF:43]

    First complete visible line 1 p. black ribbon typescript: burned fragment, 16 lines visible, 10 complete; TxU.

198. ["Slanting the broken moon to planes of light"]

    First line of 1 p. holograph manuscript: 3-line fragment appearing below "The Poet's Confession is Replied to" (see entry #147b); on other side is typed "Frank R. Reade, Esq"; NN-B.

199. ["[slen?]der, silver-gray, [?] [Ar?]temis"]

    First visible phase of 1 p. black ribbon typescript: burned fragment, 24 lines visible, 21 complete, 1 canceled; TxU.

200. ["That cried he had"]

    First visible phrase of 1 p. typescript: burned fragment, 18 lines visible, last 10 complete; entire text is typed in capitals; TxU.

201. ["time that slakes the heart that breaks"]

    First visible line of 1 p. black ribbon typescript: burned fragment, 11 lines visible, 9 complete; "William Faulkner." typed at bottom; TxU.

202. ["To a stately minuet of wind and wheat"]

    First visible line (sixth) of 1 p. purple ribbon typescript: burned fragment, 4 quatrains visible, 11 lines complete; "William Faulkner." typed at bottom; TxU.

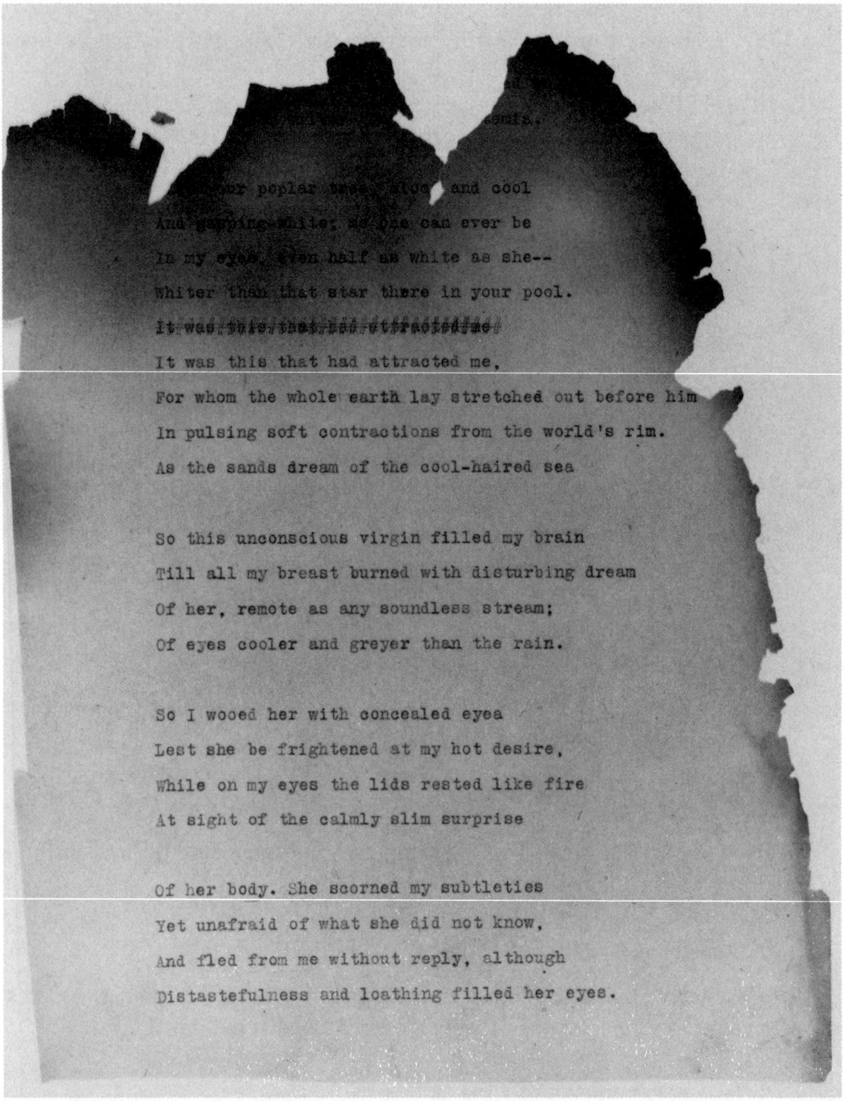

. . . . . .r poplar tree. . . .and cool
And . . . . . .-while: . . . . .can ever be
In my eyes. . . .en half as white as she--
Whiter than that star there in your pool.
It was this, that had attracted me,
It was this that had attracted me,
For whom the whole earth lay stretched out before him
In pulsing soft contractions from the world's rim.
As the sands dream of the cool-haired sea

So this unconscious virgin filled my brain
Till all my breast burned with disturbing dream
Of her, remote as any soundless stream;
Of eyes cooler and greyer than the rain.

So I wooed her with concealed eyes
Lest she be frightened at my hot desire,
While on my eyes the lids rested like fire
At sight of the calmly slim surprise

Of her body. She scorned my subtleties
Yet unafraid of what she did not know,
And fled from me without reply, although
Distastefulness and loathing filled her eyes.

Figure 42.   Unidentified, Burned Poem Fragment ["[slen?]der,
silver-gray, [?] [Ar?]temis"] (#199)
*(Courtesy Jill Faulkner Summers and the Harry Ransom
Humanities Research Center, The University of Texas, Austin)*

203. "To Spring, in Winter" [*UV:35]

   Title of 1 p. black ribbon typescript: burned fragment, 14 lines visible, 11 complete; TxU.

204. ["towers sank down the rushing west"] [*UF:55]

   Second visible and first legible line 1 p. purple ribbon typescript: burned fragment, parts of 7 lines visible; TxU.

205. ["Weave for me an evening broken"] [*UF:57]

   First visible line 1 p. black ribbon typescript: burned fragment, 4 lines complete; TxU.

206. ["When I was young and smooth of cheek"]

   First line of 4-line fragment cut from sheet and pasted to page containing separately listed ["When silver rain like a young girl grieves,"] #207; MsU (Wynn, folder 4, #24).

207. ["When silver rain like a young girl grieves"]

   First line of 1 p. typescript: burned fragment, 16 lines visible, 12 complete; at top is pasted 4-line fragment listed separately as ["When I was young and smooth of cheek,"] #206; MsU (Wynn, folder 4, #24).

208. ["While each one murmurs: Pray for me"]

   Visible phrase in 2 carbon typescripts below. Although this phrase appears in "A Dead Dancer" (#24), these typescripts are not fragments of the poem.

   a. Untitled, 1 p. carbon typescript: burned fragment, parts of 15 lines visible; 3 holograph arrows in margins; TxU.
   b. Untitled, 1 p. carbon typescript: burned fragment, 23 lines visible, 13 complete; first visible line-ends "all around / lost at sea"; TxU.

209. ["whisper of rain in woods of April"]

   First visible phrase of 1 p. typescript: burned fragment, 18 lines visible, last 10 complete; TxU.

Annotated Bibliography of Critical Writings on Faulkner's Poetry through 1987

Adams, Richard P. "The Apprenticeship of William Faulkner." *Tulane Studies in English* 12 (1962): 113–56. Rprt. in *William Faulkner: Four Decades of Criticism*. Ed. Linda Wagner (East Lansing: Michigan State University Press, 1973). 7–43.

The first criticism to note that between 1916 and 1925 William Faulkner thought of himself as a poet and that an understanding of his extensive reading and writing of poetry could illuminate his fiction. While Faulkner's own poetry is boring and derivative and manifests a disinterest in "radical experiments in modern poetic modes and techniques" (Eliot excepted), reading verse was "good for Faulkner's fiction" in which the dominant formal techniques are those normally associated with poetry. See Garrett for another intelligent early treatment of Faulkner's poetry.

_____. *Faulkner: Myth and Motion*. Princeton, New Jersey: Princeton University Press, 1968. See especially Chapter 1.

Faulkner's career was founded on the artistic aim of "demonstrating motion by stopping it," and his poetic images attempt to create this effect. However, his verse lacks the structure to assimilate these images and is further marred by "sophomoric sentimentalism," awkwardness of style, monotony, and undigested literary borrowings. Nevertheless, the imagery and rhythms of his fiction show that he "retained what he had learned, particularly in the way of imagery," during his years as a poet. Discusses the presence and effect of Faulkner's poetry in his first three novels. Specific poems treated include "L'Apres-Midi d'un Faune" (#7), *TMF,* and "The Lilacs" (#63). Also analyzes "Twilight" (#113) and "The Hill" as foreshadowing central concerns of *The Sound and the Fury*. For other readings of "The Hill" in the context of Faulkner's poetry and later fiction, see Brooks, McHaney, Marshall, *Stylization,* and others.

Aiken, Conrad. "William Faulkner: The Novel as Form." *Atlantic Monthly* 164 (November 1939): 650–54. Rprt. in *William Faulkner: Four Decades of Criticism.* Ed. Linda Wagner. East Lansing: Michigan State University Press, 1973. 134–40.

Inquiry into the origins of Faulkner's art begins here. Aiken never knew the formulative role his own poetry played in developing the novelist's style (especially Faulkner's own "symphonies in verse" like *Vision in Spring*—see *Origins,* Samway, and *Stylization*). Yet here, reviewing *The Wild Palms,* Aiken identifies those experiments in polyphony as the essence of Faulkner's novels' innovative and diverse formal structures.

Baskett, Sam S. Rev. of *Vision in Spring* and *The Origins of Faulkner's Art* by Judith L. Sensibar. *Centennial Review* 29 (October 1985): 381–82.

Extends *Origins*'s argument that "Love Song" (#64) is a parody.

Bennett, J. A. W. "Faulkner and A. E. Housman." *Notes and Queries* 27 (June 1980): 234.

A brief note adding to Cleanth Brooks's listing of Faulkner's borrowings from Housman (see Brooks 1978).

Bleikasten, André. "Faulkner before Faulkner: Masks and Mirrors." In his *The Most Splendid Failure: Faulkner's* The Sound and the Fury. Bloomington: Indiana University Press, 1976. 3–42.

Examines *TMF* as a precursor to *The Sound and the Fury:* these "slender imitations of the late romantic, decadent verse of the eighties and nineties" provide evidence of "an immature talent and nothing more," given their "tame Georgian conventionality." But the poetry does manifest "meticulous craftsmanship" and Faulkner's "incipient concern for form and structure." It suggests as well fictional themes and motifs (nature imagery, seasonal framework, pastoral mode).

———. "Pan et Pierrot, ou les premiers masques de Faulkner." *Revue de littérature comparée* 22.4 (July-September 1979): 299–310.

Decadent themes and romantic imagery, especially Swinburne's, left traces in Faulkner's work up through *Flags in the Dust.* Themes and images discussed are androgyny ("Hermaphroditus," #45); the faun (*TMF,* embodying the poet's "tortured impotence" and the prototype for Faulkner's later "sick heroes"); the "dreamer" and the "femme fatale" (Pierrot and Marietta of *TM*).

Blotner, Joseph. *Faulkner: A Biography*. 2 volumes. New York: Random House, 1974.

Provides biographical context for almost all of Faulkner's poems. See volume 1, esp. pp. 115–550 passim. For references to individual poems, see Blotner's index. See also Blotner's revised discussion of Faulkner's poetry in the 1-volume 1984 edition (New York: Random House). Poems discussed in this volume are "The Ace" (#1), p. 63; *TMF* and "L'Apres-Midi d'un Faune" (#7), p. 71; "A Dead Dancer" (#24), p. 72; "Sapphics" (#95), p. 78; "The Lilacs" (#63), p. 79; poems published in *The Mississippian*, pp. 81–84; *TMF*, pp. 93–96 and 116; *VIS*, pp. 96–98; "Two Puppets in a Fifth Avenue Win[dow?]" (#114), p. 107; "Mississippi Hills: My Epitaph" (#70) and *MP*, pp. 123–24; "November 11th" (#75), p. 137; *HC*, pp. 151–52; "Cathedral in the Rain" (#129), p. 166; "Ode to the Louver" (#76), pp. 169–70; *VIS* and *HC*, p. 173; and *AGB*, pp. 315–16.

———— . Introduction. *Mississippi Poems*. By William Faulkner. Oxford, Mississippi: Yoknapatawpha Press, 1979. 1–9. Rprt. in *Helen: A Courtship and Mississippi Poems*. New Orleans and Oxford, Mississippi: Tulane University Press and Yoknapatwapha Press. 131–48.

Gives the provenance of the poems and includes a brief account of Faulkner's long friendship with Myrtle Ramey, the woman to whom he presented this carbon typescript of *MP* in October 1924. Suggests a thematic progression in the poems and some potentially illuminating relations between the discrete lyrics. Faulkner's Housman-like verse in *MP* is "strongly anti-modernist." Note: Blotner published this introduction *before* the Wynn Collection was made available to the public. Thus he does not discuss the earlier Wynn version of *MP*.

———— . "Sole Owner and Proprieter." In *Faulkner: Fifty Years After* The Marble Faun. Ed. George H. Wolfe. University, Alabama: University of Alabama Press, 1976. 1–20.

Biographical interpretation of the early poetry: poems such as "L'Apres-Midi d'un Faune" (#7), *TMF*, and "The Lilacs" (#63) evidence Faulkner's turning to art in the face of personal disappointments.

Bonner, Thomas, Jr. Introduction. *William Faulkner: The William B. Wisdom Collection: A Descriptive Catalogue*. New Orleans: Tulane University Libraries, 1980. 1–7.

Describes the general contents of the collection; summarizes the themes of *Mayday* (1926) and *HC* (1926), the two books Faulkner gave to Helen Baird Lyman; and describes the contents of several letters Faulkner wrote to her. Transcribes and comments briefly on ["Behind the mask—a maiden's face"] (#11) and ["She is like a tower of warm ivory"] (#98).

Boozer, William. *William Faulkner's First Book:* The Marble Faun *Fifty Years Later*. Memphis: Pigeon Roost Press, 1974, 1975.

Catalogues all known copies of *TMF*, gives the book's history at auction, traces its rise in value in rare book catalogues, and provides a selective bibliography.

Bosha, Francis J. *Faulkner's* Soldiers' Pay: *A Bibliographic Study*. Troy, New York: Whitston, 1982. See pp. 3–13.

Soldiers' Pay originated in some of Faulkner's early poetry. "The Lilacs" (#63) and "November 11" (#75), the novel's epigraph, relate to the novel thematically. See Yonce 1983 for essay review of this work.

Brodsky, Louis Daniel. "Additional Manuscripts of Faulkner's 'A Dead Dancer.'" *SB* 34 (1981): 267–70.

Building from Crane and Freudenberg's description of "A Dead Dancer" (#24) in *Man Collecting,* Brodsky discusses versions of the poem in his private collection. He includes lines from several drafts as well as his "reconstructions."

———. "The Autograph Manuscripts of Faulkner's 'The Lilacs.'" *SB* 36 (1983): 240–52.

Transcribes seven holograph fragments of "The Lilacs" (#63) from Brodsky's private collection and the ViU collection; prints the 3-page pencil draft of the poem; collates it against the fair ink copy on the other side; and transcribes *The Lilacs* version in order to postulate an order of composition.

———. "Elder Watson in Heaven": Poet Faulkner as Satirist." *Faulkner Journal* 1.1 (Fall 1985): 2–7.

Publishes and comments on typescript of poem (#29) from Brodsky's private collection. The poem reveals Faulkner's interest in E. A. Robinson.

———. "Eunice." *MissQ* 31 (Summer 1978): 449–52.

Transcribes, gives provenance of, and comments on significance of "Eunice" (#33).

——— and Robert W. Hamblin. "Faulkner's 'L'Apres-Midi d'un Faune': The Evolution of a Poem." *SB* 33 (1980): 254–63.

Catalogues the changes made in successive drafts of "L'Apres-Midi d'un Faune" (#7) and comments on their significance.

Brodsky, Louis Daniel and Robert W. Hamblin, eds. *Faulkner: A Comprehensive Guide to the Brodsky Collection.* Vol. I: *The Biobibliography* and Vol. II: *The Letters.* Jackson: University Press of Mississippi, 1982 and 1984.

Vol. I lists all Faulkner poetry manuscripts and typescripts in Brodsky's private collection (see short-title listing *H/B 1982*) and gives the provenance and publication history of Brodsky's Faulkner acquisitions. Also prints photoreproductions of selected manuscripts and typescripts. Vol. II includes letters relating to Faulkner's poetry. See especially entries 39 (p. 3), 55 (p. 5), 245a–b (pp. 8–12), 1503h–i (pp. 294–97), and 1557a–b (pp. 302–305), an exchange between Richard P. Adams and Phil Stone concerning Faulkner's poetry. The comprehensive guides include all information from earlier catalogues given in the short-title listings above. [*Note: At press time, I was informed that a revised edition of these volumes was being prepared.*]

———. "William Faulkner: Poet at Large." *SoR* 18 (October 1982): 767–75.

Transcribes manuscript copy of Faulkner's poem "Pregnacy" (#87) and gives provenance.

Brooks, Cleanth. "Faulkner as Poet." *Southern Literary Journal* 1 (December 1968): 5–19.

An earlier version of the chapters in Brooks 1978.

———. "The Image of Helen Baird in Faulkner's Early Poetry and Fiction." *SR* 85.2 (Spring 1977): 218–234.

A more detailed version of Brooks's 1978 discussion (pp. 47–60) of Faulkner's romantic "fascination with the unattainable" in his poetry and early fiction. Faulkner fictionalizes the images of himself as thwarted poet and lover and of Helen Baird as fatal temptress. Includes a brief but revealing paragraph on Meta Carpenter Wilde. Poems discussed are those in *HC*. (See also Brooks's note in *Bonner:* 15–16.)

———. *Toward Yoknapatawpha and Beyond*. New Haven and London: Yale University Press, 1978. See especially 1–66 and 345–63.

"The bonds that rendered [Faulkner] relatively 'mute and impotent' were not marble but literary." His verse was essentially "empty and sterile." Charts Faulkner's poetic imitations and transformations and notes significant borrowings from Housman, Eliot, Verlaine, Swinburne, Tennyson, Rostand, Cummings, Shakespeare, Keats, Yeats, and others. While Faulkner's self-apprenticeship to poetry was both extensive and important, his poetry is flawed by a lack of authenticity due to its excessive literariness and by its lack of focus. Faulkner needed the "more ample form of fiction to bring his 'poetry' to full fruition." Even relatively successful poems such as *AGB* II (#69), III (#37), IV (#41), VI (#6), and XLIV (#68) become "more massively rich and convincing as developed in the prose-poetry of one of his stories." Discussion includes other poems from *AGB,* as well as *TMF,* "Hymn" (#49), "Aubade" (#9), "L'Apres-Midi d'un Faune" (#7), Faulkner's Verlaine translations (#19, 34, 18, and 104), and "Love Song" (#64). Illustrates the differences between the poetry and prose by comparing *AGB* IV (#41) and XXX (#48) to *Soldiers' Pay* and by comparing *AGB* XLIV (#68) to the "prose hymn" which concludes "The Bear"; by discussing parallels between images in the poetry and in *The Hamlet;* and by examining poetic diction in the novels (see Notes on "Miss Rosa Coldfield's Poetry," pp. 354–61). Chapter 2 explores the "depth and quality" of Faulkner's romanticism as seen in *TM* and in *HC*.

Broughton, Panthea Reid. "An Interview with Meta Carpenter Wilde." *SoR* 18 (Fall 1982): 776–801.

Wilde expands on her memoir account (see Wilde) of Faulkner's reading, writing, and reciting his own and others' poetry to her as part of their courtship and provides evidence of the role poetry played in Faulkner's life long after he had "abandoned" it. Wilde's comments on the nature of their affair suggest why Faulkner brought his "failed poet's voice" to all his recorded romantic relationships.

Brown, Calvin S. "These Thirteen Faulkner Books." *SR* 94.1 (Winter 1986): 167–80.

Faulkner's "Sapphics" (#95) is a "poor imitation, verging on plagiarism." Its bungled metrics prove that he had no understanding of the Sapphic stanza. His attempts to imitate Aiken's metrics were similarly awkward; there, too, he was trying to imitate something that he did not understand.

Collins, Carvel. "Biographical Background for Faulkner's *Helen.*" In *Helen: A Courtship and Mississippi Poems.* By William Faulkner. New Orleans and Oxford, Mississippi: Tulane University Press and Yoknapatawpha Press, 1981. 9–105.

An introduction to the sonnet sequence. The 16 poems have a "logical sequential arrangement." Gives the textual history and biographical significance of each poem and points to the poems' later use in Faulkner's fiction. Many assertions are undocumented so factual information and resulting interpretations are problematic, but account of Faulkner's friendship with Helen Baird—to whom he gave this sonnet sequence—and discussion provide the most extensive treatment of *HC* to date.

_____ . "Faulkner at the University of Mississippi." In his *William Faulkner: Early Prose and Poetry.* Boston: Little, Brown and Company, 1962. 3–33.

An undocumented account of Faulkner's literary activities at the University of Mississippi from 1916 to 1925, the period during which he wrote the poems, essays, and fiction and made the drawings printed in this collection.

_____ . Introduction. *Mayday.* By William Faulkner. Notre Dame, Indiana: University of Notre Dame Press, 1976. 3–41.

Introduction deals primarily with Faulkner's 1926 prose fable but includes a brief comparison of *HC* and *Mayday,* both of which were written for and given to Helen Baird in 1926.

Crane, Joan St. C. "Faulkner's *The Marble Faun* Redivivus: An Idle Conjecture." *American Book Collector* 4.5 (September-October 1983): 11–22.

Conjectures on the printing and circulation history of *TMF.*

Delgarno, Emily. "Faulkner's Pierrot." *Notes on Mississippi Writers* 14.2 (1982): 73–76.

Pierrot's song in *TM* echoes lines from Robert Nichols's "Plaint of Pierrot Ill-Used" in *Ardours and Endurances.* Faulkner differed from Eliot,

Pound, and Crane in deriving his Pierrot from Verlaine rather than LaForgue. Delgarno's suggestion that Faulkner did not know his fellow modernists' Pierrot poems seems unlikely as Faulkner paraphrases Eliot in *TM*. For other comparisons to Nichols, see Kreisworth 1980 and *Stylization*.

Folks, Jeffrey F. "The Influence of Poetry on the Narrative Technique of Faulkner's Early Fiction." *The Journal of Narrative Technique* 9 (1979): 184–90.

Discusses the poetry's stylistic and thematic influence on Faulkner's treatment of time and space, his constant juxtapositions of highly stylized decadent or romantic structures with realistic and modernist formal structures, and his interest in the isolated and isolating consciousness. *TMF*'s 5-part temporal structure underlies the structures of several early novels, and many fictional figures are more successful reworkings of the romantic protagonist in Faulkner's poetry. In summary, Faulkner assumed "the modernists' anti-romantic stance within an underlying romantic structure." See Brooks 1978 for similar view and *Stylization* for extension and expansion of this thesis. Includes brief discussion of gardens in Faulkner's poetry and fiction (see also Polk and Simpson) and of the particular difficulties facing a Southern would-be modernist.

Garrett, George P., Jr. "An Examination of the Poetry of William Faulkner." *Princeton University Library Chronicle* 18.3 (Spring 1957): 124–35. Rprt. in *Four Decades of Criticism*. Ed. Linda Wagner. East Lansing: Michigan State University Press, 1973. 44–54.

Refutes dismissive treatments of Faulkner's poetry and argues for *TMF*'s complex sequential arrangement. The poems go beyond imitation and are experimental in ways that foreshadow Faulkner's mature narrative techniques. Besides defending *TMF*, Garrett compares the *Contempo* version and the *AGB* version (XXXVI) of "Spring" (#103) to illustrate Faulkner's concern with revision. Also discusses the "variety of form and subject matter," using *AGB* XIX (#27), XIV (#38), XXXIV (#100), X (#113), and XLIV (#70) to illustrate.

Gresset, Michel. *Faulkner ou la fascination: Poétique du Regard*. Paris: Klincksieck, 1982. See especially pp. 11–66.

Focuses on the development of Faulkner's "visual poetics" up to 1936. "Mississippi Hills: My Epitaph" (#70) and the prose poem "Carcassonne" mark the division between Faulkner's early period of "hesitation" (1919–

24)—professional, geographical and psychological—and a period of "choice" (1924–36)—Faulkner's return to his literal and fictive "homeland." Thus the 1919, 1924 *TMF* is a derivative work in which Faulkner substitutes aesthetic contemplation for participation. The faun is Faulkner's first "voyeur," but a voyeur freed from guilt by his imprisonment in stone. The later *AGB* brings this paralyzed vision to life, enriching and correcting *TMF*. *AGB*, a "spiritual autobiography," manifests the essential ethical issues of Faulkner's art. This explains why Faulkner published the collection in 1933, after he had written several major novels.

————. "The 'God' of Faulkner's Fiction." In *Faulkner and Idealism: Perspectives from Paris*. Eds. Michel Gresset and Patrick Samway, S.J. Jackson: University Press of Mississippi, 1983. 51–70.

Investigating the "*lexis* of idealism" in Faulkner's art within the dual contexts of Mallarmé and psychoanalysis, Gresset locates its earliest manifestations in Faulkner's poetry and early fiction. No specific poems discussed.

Gwynn, F. L. "Faulkner's Prufrock—and Other Observations." *Journal of English and Germanic Philology* 52 (January 1953): 63–70.

Notes Eliot's influence on *AGB* I (#63), II (#69), and XXVII (#92) and *Mosquitoes*. Faulkner's literary satire of Eliot's Prufrockian figures is "heavy-handed."

Hamblin, Robert W. "*The Marble Faun:* Chapter One of Faulkner's Continuing Dialectic on Life and Art." *Publications of the Missouri Philological Association* 3 (1978): 80–90.

TMF manifests Faulkner's early and sustained interest in the antithetical relationship between art and life. The young poet's apprenticeship work centers on the marble-bound faun's desire to escape his existence as an immortal but lifeless work of art and to enter experience, imaged by personified nature; Faulkner the novelist reconciles this antithesis in a "living literature."

Harrison, Robert. *Aviation Lore in Faulkner*. Amsterdam and Philadelphia: John Benjamins, 1985.

Provides a brief biographical note concerning Faulkner's fascination with aviation and a glossary of aviation terms appearing in his fiction and poetry, including *AGB* I (#63) and XVIII (#25).

Hönnighausen, Lothar. "Faulkner's First Published Poem: 'L'Apres-Midi d'un Faune.'" *William Faulkner: Materials, Studies, and Criticism* 6.1 (May 1984): 1–19.

An expanded discussion of material included in *Stylization,* chapter 3 which covers the following poems in greater detail: "Fantouches" (#34), "Une Ballade des Femmes Perdues" (#10), "L'Apres-Midi d'un Faune" (#7), and "Naiads' Song" (#73).

———. "Faulkner's Poetry." *REAL: Yearbook of Research in English and American Literature* 2 (1984): 355–69.

A bibliographic essay which cites and summarizes much of the work on Faulkner's poetry to 1982. A selective introduction to critical studies of Faulkner's verse.

———. "The Role of Swinburne and Eliot in Faulkner's Literary Development." *Amerikastudien/American Studies (AMST)* 28.4 (1983): 467–83.

An early version of parts of *Stylization,* chapter 4, which includes the assertion (dropped from *Stylization*), that A. E. Housman's influence on Faulkner's poetry did not exert itself until well after Faulkner had worked through his Swinburne and Eliot phase.

———. *William Faulkner: The Art of Stylization in His Early Graphic and Literary Work.* Cambridge: Cambridge University Press, 1987.

Analyzes the relationship between Faulkner's early artwork and poetry and his later, lyrical prose style. Faulkner's early artwork and poetry serve as a training ground and a touchstone for the fiction of a novelist whose "specific artistic genius lies in the productive tension between the concreteness of realistic description and various means of stylization" (see Folks and others for a similar argument, but Hönnighausen is the first to focus on all of Faulkner's artwork and to provide a detailed, historically and culturally oriented study of his iconography). Faulkner's early poetry, prose fiction, and art owe debts to the late romantic and early modernist movements but diverge in significant ways from their precursors (see also Brooks 1978 and *Origins*). His apparently anomalous artwork—his drawings and hand-crafted books—bears hitherto unnoted similarities to that of other young aspiring artists of his generation. Central to Faulkner's "mode of vision" in the early work is the Pierrot mask. Includes many illustrative plates. Dismisses other scholarly work on Faulkner's art and poetry as "influence studies" and "biographical treatments." Poem sequences discussed are *AGB, HC, The Lilacs, TMF, VIS,* and the [*Estelle Poems*]. For discussion of individual poems within sequences and lyrics, see *Stylization* index.

Kenner, Hugh. "The Last Novelist." In his *A Homemade World: The American Modernist Writers.* New York: William Morrow, 1975. 194–221. See especially 194–98.

Faulkner's early poetry and drawings show his "Mississippi aestheticism" deriving from the decadents: "The savageries his blood-saturated rustics ritualize are of frozen Art Nouveau sumptuousness." Quotes from poems published in *EPP* and *TMF* to suggest resonances between the Symbolists' (especially Mallarmé's) and Faulkner's aesthetics.

Kinney, Arthur R. and Doreen Fowler. "Faulkner's Rowan Oak Papers: A Census." *JML* 10 (June 1983): 327–34.

Lists by acquisition number materials found in a closet at Rowan Oak in 1971, temporarily deposited at ViU, and now at MsU. Among these Faulkner papers is some poetry. The authors write that the papers' excellent state of preservation suggests that "they were meant to be archival" as Faulkner "expected the study of his work to continue and his legacy to memorialize the stages of composition."

Kreisworth, Martin. "Faulkner as Translator: His Versions of Verlaine." *MissQ* 30 (Summer 1977): 429–32.

Faulkner's four Verlaine poems, "Fantouches" (#34), "Clair de Lune" (#18), "Streets" (#104), and "A Clymene" (#19), are "fairly literal" translations and suggest his reliance on earlier translations by Arthur Symons. The final line of "Fantouches," an allusion borrowed from Eliot (see also Brooks 1978), provides a "self-conscious and sophisticated comment on poetic translation and literary borrowing."

————. "Faulkner's *The Marble Faun:* Dependence and Independence." *English Studies in Canada* 6.3 (Fall 1980): 333–44.

Discusses the similarities between Robert Nichols' "A Faun's Holiday" and Faulkner's "L'Apres-Midi d'un Faune" (#7), *AGB* XXXIII (#57), "Naiads' Song" (#73), and *TMF*. The unpublished 1920 *TMF* typescript shows Faulkner "dramatically" reshaping "the traditional pastoral cycle to conform to his own conception of literary form": the lyrics in *TMF* "remain fundamentally separate units." (See Garrett and *Origins* for differing views.)

————. *William Faulkner: The Making of a Novelist*. Athens: University of Georgia Press, 1983. See especially 1–36.

First chapter summarizes his two earlier articles on Faulkner the poet. Influenced by Willard Huntington Wright's *The Creative Will,* Faulkner self-consciously imitated other poets in a deliberate apprenticeship program. This resulted in "creative re-workings" (not mere imitations) of Swinburne in "Sapphics" (#95) and *AGB* XXXVIII (#45); of Housman in *AGB* VIII through XI (#43, 106, 113, and 117); of Eliot in "Love Song" (#64) and "The Lilacs" (#63); and of Robert Nichols in *TMF.* Chapter 2 compares the pastoral in "The Hill" to "Sapphics" (#95) and "Twilight" (#113).

Lind, Ilse Dusoir. "Faulkner and Nature." *Faulkner Studies, An Annual of Research, Criticism, and Reviews.* Ed. Barnett Guttenberg. Coral Gables: Department of English, University of Miami, 1980. 112–21.

A general essay on the origins and development of Faulkner's fictional representations of nature. *TMF* is "a tone poem." There, especially in describing the natural world, "the reverse of imagism is the intent": in his deliberately literary, antirealistic nature descriptions, Faulkner rejected imagism in favor of symbolism. See *Stylization* and Wagner 1976 for alternative readings.

Marshall, Alexander, III. "William Faulkner: The Symbolist Connection." *American Literature* 59 (October 1987): 389–401.

Faulkner's interest in symbolist aesthetics and techniques first manifested itself in his adaptation of the Pierrot and faun personas, his early Verlaine (via Symons) adaptations, and his Mallarmé imitation. This interest bears fruit in the stylistic and thematic concerns of his best fiction. (See also Brooks, Polk, *Origins, Stylization,* and others.) Examines the symbolist infusion in Faulkner's poetry and fiction and notes its place in Faulkner's aesthetics. Poems discussed are "L'Apres-Midi d'un Faune" (#7), "Clair de Lune" (#18), *TMF, TM,* "A Clymene" (#19), "Pierrot, Sitting Beside the Body of the Dead Columbine" (#83), and "Une Ballade des Femmes Perdues" (#10). Discusses influence of Faulkner's poetry on "The Hill" and Ike's cow "escapade" (see Brooks 1978 and Kreisworth 1983).

McHaney, Thomas. "The Development of Faulkner's Idealism: Hands, Horses, Whores." In *Faulkner and Idealism: Perspectives from Paris.* Eds. Michel Gresset and Patrick Samway, S.J. Jackson: University Press of Mississippi, 1983. 71–85.

The faun and naiad are central images in Faulkner's po~
former transforms to a horse and the latter to a whore in his
Poems mentioned briefly are *TMF,* "Cathay" (#16), "After 1.
(#4), "Naiads' Song" (#73), and Faulkner's early sketches (prose
"The Hill," "Nympholepsy," and "Carcassone."

Meriwether, James B. "Faulkner's 'Ode to the Louver.'" *MissQ* 27 (Summer 1974): 333–35.

Transcribes and gives provenance of "Ode to the Louver" (#76) and the letter to Phil Stone in which the poem was enclosed.

———. "'Pierrot, Sitting Beside the Body of Columbine, Suddenly Sees Himself in a Mirror." *MissQ* 35 (Summer 1982): 305–8.

Transcribes and gives provenance and "conjectural—though quite probable" dating of the poem. Information differs from that given in *H/B 1982:* 17, and casts doubt on Brodsky's claim that this poem is part of the [*Aunt Bama Poems*].

Millgate, Michael. *The Achievement of William Faulkner.* Lincoln: University of Nebraska Press, 1963, 1978.

His opening chapter, "The Career" (1–57), remains one of the most concise, accurate, and well documented chronological accounts of Faulkner's early career as a poet. His description of Faulkner's New Orleans phase, in particular of his relations with Sherwood Anderson and discussion of Faulkner's familiarity—or lack thereof—with Joyce's *Ulysses,* is especially valuable.

———. "Starting out in the Twenties: Reflections on *Soldiers' Pay." Mosaic* 7.1 (Fall 1973): 1–14.

This reading of *Soldiers' Pay* expands Millgate's comments in *Achievement* and includes a discussion of the relation of poetry—specific poems and formal techniques—to Faulkner's first published novel. Faulkner's imagination was "saturated with the language, rhythms, patterns, and images of late romanticism." Poems discussed are "November 11" (#75), *TMF, AGB* XXXIII (#57), and "Adolescence" (#2).

Minter, David. *William Faulkner: His Life and Work.* Baltimore: Johns Hopkins University Press, 1980. See chapters 1–3, especially pp. 24-25, and chapter 7, especially pp. 160–64.

This biography briefly analyzes the psychological import of Faulkner's poetry and drawings and notes their role in the author's relationships with various women he loved. Faulkner's poetry was not a source for his originality: by 1920 it was already becoming a "dead end." Sometimes asserts suppositions as fact (that Faulkner's lost "Orpheus" manuscript was a revision of *Vision in Spring*) and gives datings that are problematic (the [*Estelle Poems*]). Poems discussed in any detail are *TMF, TM,* and ["Red thy famble"] (#93).

Morton, Bruce. "The Irony and Significance of Two Early Faulkner and Hemingway Poems Appearing in the *Double Dealer.*" *Zeitschrift für Anglistik und Amerikanistik* 3 (1980): 254–58.

A stylistic and thematic comparison of "Portrait" (#86) and Hemingway's early poem "Ultimately," both of which were published on the same page of the June 1922 issue of the *Double Dealer* and in *Salmagundi*. The two poems offer a "primary comparative resource" and prove conclusively that as early as 1922 both writers were aware not only of each others' existence but of their profound aesthetic differences.

Mulqueen, James. "Horace Benbow: Avatar of Faulkner's Marble Faun." *Notes on Mississippi Writers* 9 (1976): 88–96.

A thematic reading of the Horace Benbow of both *Flags in the Dust* and *Sanctuary* as a fictional version of Faulkner's Marble Faun, "trapped forever in repellant reality."

O'Connor, William Van. "William Faulkner's Apprenticeship." *Southwest Review* 38 (Winter 1953): 1–14.

An early account of Faulkner's poetic apprenticeship, 1918–26. Quotes and discusses the *NR* version of "L'Apres-Midi d'un Faune" (#7) and "The Lilacs" (#63) in relation to Faulkner's first three novels.

Onoe, Masaji. "Some T. S. Eliot Echoes in Faulkner." In *Faulkner Studies in Japan*. Comp. by Kenzaburo Ohashi and Kiyoyuki Ono and ed. by Thomas L. McHaney. Athens: University of Georgia Press, 1985. 45–61.

Discusses Faulkner's choice of Eliotic rather than Shakespearean "verbal echoes" in *AGB* II (#70), III (#38), and XXV (#31).

Page, Sally R. *Faulkner's Women: Characterization and Meaning.* Deland, Florida: Everett/Edwards, 1972. See especially 1–3 and 11–17.

Chapter 1, "The Lure of Sex and Modern Alienation," connects the image of women in the *EPP* poems and in *TMF* to the image of women in Faulkner's early novels. *TMF* shows the "polarity between the male and female conditions" that is found in Faulkner's fiction. Specific poems discussed briefly are "Study" (#105), "L'Apres-Midi d'un Faune" (#7), and "To a Co-ed" (#109).

Pitavy, François. "Faulkner poète." *Etudes anglaises* 29.3 (1976): 456–67.

For Faulkner, the poet is driven to creativity by a "dream of beauty" that may transcend and reshape reality. *TMF, AGB* XXXVI (#103), and "Hymn" (#49) express Faulkner's ideas about and obsession with this (Keatsian) dream. Faulkner's poetic vision reaches fruition when he turns to prose (beginning with "Carcassonne") and finds the space to transcribe both the objects of the poetic quest and the quest itself.

Polk, Noel. Introduction. *The Marionettes.* By William Faulkner. Charlottesville: University Press of Virginia, 1977. ix–xxxii and appendices.

Provides textual apparatus for and first full-length analysis of this 1920 hand-printed, illustrated, and bound dream-play. *TM* "flatly predicts many of the techniques" of Faulkner's fiction. Disagrees with Millgate 1963 (see also *Stylization*), who argued that *TM*'s chief importance is its "combination of text and illustrations" and its "overall stylization of language, action, and line." Argues, rather, that its "literary qualities," its revelations about Faulkner's aesthetics, and its achievements "as a work of art in itself" are its significance. Notes early textual connection between *TM* and *TMF* (see also Sensibar 1979), details and analyzes influences, and suggests thematic foreshadowings of Faulkner's novels. Poems discussed are *TMF*, "Clair de Lune" (#18), "Two Puppets in a Fifth Avenue Win[dow?]" (#114), and ["Those cries like sca[ttered silve?]r sails"] (#108).

Pruvot, Monique. "Faulkner and the Voices of Orphism." In *Faulkner and Idealism: Perspectives from Paris.* Eds. Michel Gresset and Patrick Samway, S.J. Jackson: University Press of Mississippi, 1983. 127–43.

Mythic conceptions, particularly the Orphic myth, are central to Faulkner's fiction. Faulkner first explores these myths in his poetry. Poems discussed are "Orpheus" (#80), "Une Ballade des Femmes Perdues" (#10), and "Cathay" (#16).

Putzel, Max. *Genius of Place: William Faulkner's Triumphant Beginnings.* Baton Rouge: Louisiana State University Press, 1985. 1–26.

Faulkner's imaginative beginnings are found in his short stories, not his poetry—which contributed little, if anything, to Faulkner's growth as a writer. "How did such a foppish minor poet ever turn himself into the titanic man of letters. . . . What godlike power drove away the flatulent muse of his poesy. . .?"

Richardson, H. Edward. "The Decadence in Faulkner's First Novel: The Faun, the Worm, and the Tower." *Etudes anglaises* 21.3 (July-September 1968): 225–35.

Like *Soldiers' Pay,* the early poetry and *TMF* were influenced by the decadents and French symbolists.

———. *William Faulkner: The Journey to Self-Discovery.* Columbia: University of Missouri Press, 1969. See especially 38–138.

Romantic, French symbolist, and Elizabethan poetry influenced *TMF,* a sequence that allowed Faulkner to "probe his problems romantically, mythically and symbolically," particularly his sense of being "marble-bound" in the past of his own South. Lyrics from the early 1920s fall into three categories: experiments in traditional verse forms, symbolist poems, and poems related to *TMF. AGB* points toward Faulkner's movement away from romantic devices and toward "possession of his own region." Poems discussed in detail include "Boy and Eagle" (#25), *TMF,* "Sapphics" (#95), "Cathay" (#16), "Portrait" (#86), and "Nocturne" (#123).

Rossi-Bouchrara, Beatrice. "Le style d'un poète manqué." *L'Arc: Revue Trimestrielle* 84–85 (1983): 29–37.

While there is a great dichotomy between Faulkner the poet and Faulkner the novelist, Faulkner's experience as a poet is the mainspring of his novelistic creative genius. Includes a general discussion of poems published in *EPP* but focuses on *TMF* and *TM. TM* represents a "cross-roads of crisis." Pierrot, a man who falls and flies is the "creator of the spectacle of his own frustration." The play articulates itself around three moments of desire: attraction, seduction, and the fall.

Runyan, Harry. "Faulkner's Poetry." *Faulkner Studies* 3.2–3 (Summer-Autumn 1954): 23–39.

Catalogues the "56 pieces" of Faulkner's "extant poetry" and dismisses them as the work of a beginning writer, almost wholly derivative in nature and marked by an "immature romanticism."

Samway, Patrick, S.J. "Faulkner's Poetic Vision." In *Faulkner and the Southern Renaissance.* Ed. Doreen Fowler and Ann J. Abadie. Jackson: University Press of Mississippi, 1982. 204–44.

The returning soldier's plight; the quest for an illusive, ideal woman and her subsequent loss; the role of the poet; and the acceptance of solitude and death were the "concerns" of Faulkner's poetry. Discusses literary influences and departures from them and suggests thematic relationships among various poems, particularly those in *VIS, AGB,* and *TM.* Liberal quotations from a variety of poems.

Sensibar, Judith L. Introduction. *Vision in Spring.* By William Faulkner. Austin: University of Texas Press, 1984. ix–xxviii.

Provides information about the original 1921 manuscript and related fragments and reviews and, in some cases, enlarges the discussion of *VIS* in *Origins.* The sequence shows Faulkner attempting modernist techniques in an extended piece of work a full 4 years before he wrote his first novel. Its form and content anticipate the shape and style of *Soldiers' Pay, The Sound and the Fury, Light in August,* and other fiction. Text (fourteen poems) includes nine poems published for the first time.

————. *The Origins of Faulkner's Art.* Austin: University of Texas Press, 1984. Chapter 12 condensed in *William Faulkner: Modern Critical Views.* Ed. Harold Bloom. New York: Chelsea House, 1986. 269–79.

This first full-length study analyzes Faulkner's early, transparently autobiographical poetry; explores what being a poet meant to him; and clarifies the relation of his long poetic apprenticeship to his novelistic career. Faulkner's early work is integrally related to the later masterpieces. Through his imitations, dialogues with, and parodies of other poets (especially Swinburne, Mallarmé, Aiken, and Eliot), Faulkner was inventing and learning to control structures, techniques, and attitudes that would prove central to his fiction. His three major poem sequences and the dreamplay, *TM,* manifest two emergent organizing principles—consistent employment of the Pierrot mask and steady use of cyclical poetic forms.

Ultimately, his poetic apprenticeship enables Faulkner to emerge from the welter of others' voices—ancestral and literary—to become the sole proprietor of his own imaginative life. Works treated in detail are *The Lilacs, TMF, VIS,* and *TM.* For individual poems within these sequences and complete listing of the discrete lyrics discussed, see *Origins* index.

––––––. *"Pierrot and The Marble Faun:* Another Fragment." *MissQ* 32 (Summer 1979): 473–76.

Transcribes the 44-line fragment beginning "Your little feet have crossed my heart" (#108), which Faulkner wrote on 3 blank pages at the end of his first-edition copy of Ralph Hodgson's *Poems;* discusses its provenance; and notes its relation to the two 2-page typescript fragments informally collated and transcribed by Polk beginning ["Those cries, like scatt[ered silve?]r sails"]. These fragments (#108c) provide further evidence that the Marble Faun and Pierrot at one time shared a single lyric.

––––––. "William Faulkner, Poet to Novelist: An Imposter Becomes an Artist." In *Psychoanalytic Studies of Biography.* Ed. by George Moraitis, M.D. and George H. Pollock, M.D., Ph.D. Monograph 4 of the Emotions and Behavior Monograph Series of the Chicago Institute for Psychoanalysis. Madison, Connecticut: International University Press, 1987. 221–49.

An enlarged and more psychoanalyticaly focused treatment of material in *Origins,* chapter 4. See also Strauss.

Simpson, Lewis P. "Faulkner and the Legend of the Artist." In *Faulkner: Fifty Years After* The Marble Faun. Ed. George H. Wolfe. University, Alabama: University of Alabama Press, 1976. 69–100.

Faulkner begins to work out the self-conscious romantic legend of the literary artist in *TMF.* Specifically, he explores the modern (Southern) cultural dialectic in order to write his own version of the myth of creativity. Central to his interpretation of that dialectic is the creativity myth as it relates to Pan/Christ. Works discussed are *TMF* and *TM,* "Hermaphroditus" (#45), early prose works, and Faulkner's first four novels.

––––––. "Faulkner and the Southern Symbolism of Pastoral." *MissQ* 28 (Fall 1975): 401–16.

In the context of his larger discussion of Southern pastoral, Simpson argues that *TMF* is a "carefully constructed exercise in pastoral, ironically implying the rejection of pastoral by modernity." The mute and frozen faun, "isolated in his own consciousness," stands in a "dispossessed garden . . . a tortured creature of Pan, locked in himself like Prufrock."

Stone, Phil. Preface. *The Marble Faun*. Boston: The Four Seas Co., 1924. Rprt. in *The Marble Faun and A Green Bough*. New York: Random House, 1965. 6–8.

TMF bears the "defects of youth." Nevertheless, the poems, and the poet, "show promise."

Stonum, Gary Lee. "Visionary Poetics." In his *Faulkner's Career: An Internal Literary History*. Ithaca and London: Cornell University Press, 1979. 41–60.

Faulkner's "failure" as a poet was caused by his own "visionary poetics." Believing that poetry should express an ultimately inexpressible absolute, Faulkner narrowed himself to using symbols from the "poetic pastoral" (e.g., unreal, universal landscapes, fauns, and nymphlike maidens) which were meant to point beyond themselves toward transcendence. Failing this, Faulkner had two choices—to renounce the "absolute," as he does in his Housman-influenced poems, or to focus on the desire for peaceful oblivion, as he does in poems such as ["Admonishes his heart"] (#126) and "Orpheus" (#80). The "need to find an alternative to the suicidal longings of the visionary poet and to create an artistic space that makes room for life . . . empowers Faulkner's search for a new artistic method." (See Simpson for a different interpretation of Faulkner's "pastoral" vision.)

Storey, Robert. Rev. of *The Origins of Faulkner's Art* and *Vision in Spring* by Judith L. Sensibar. *Comparative Literature Studies* 22.4 (Winter 1985): 559–61.

Questions whether "Love Song" (#64) is a successful parody.

Strauss, Dr. Harvey. "A Discussion of Judith L. Sensibar's 'William Faulkner, Poet to Novelist: An Imposter Becomes an Artist.'" In *Psychoanalytic Studies of Biography*. Ed. by George Moraitis, M.D. and George H. Pollock, M.D., Ph.D. Monograph 4 of the Emotions and Behavior Monograph Series of the Chicago Institute for Psychoanalysis. Madison, Connecticut: International University Press, 1987. 337–46.

A psychiatrist and psychoanalyst, Strauss extends Sensibar 1987. Faulkner's roleplaying and poetic apprenticeship served both psychic and creative functions. His poetry was poor, in part, because he was more interested in becoming and being a poet than in writing great verse. His costumes, his imitative poems, and the actual books he crafted manifest an element of play but also stem from his need to create "a self concept" out of his imagination and to make this creation tangible. Ultimately, Faulkner's gratifying relationships with Phil Stone and Sherwood Anderson, who were closer to his ego ideal than was his father, freed him to value his imagination enough "to find and use his own voice to tell what he knew."

Wagner, Linda W. *Hemingway and Faulkner: Inventors/Masters*. Metuchen, New Jersey: Scarecrow Press, 1975.

Focuses on the use Faulkner made of his reading during his apprenticeship years. Unlike Hemingway, who embraced the sparseness of the imagists and vorticists, Faulkner, like Aiken, appreciated the "cumulative effects of language" and toward that end employed repetition and "musical forms" rather than depending solely on central images. The success of *AGB* lies in Faulkner's arrangement of the poems so that each poem's position within the unified collection adds to the poem's effectiveness.

————. "The Poetry in American Fiction." *Prospects: Annual of American Cultural Studies* 2 (1976): 513–26.

Faulkner, Hemingway, and Dos Passos all began as poets. The atmosphere of reciprocity between the crafting of poetry and fiction which existed in the "less genre-tied" 1920s, coupled with the prevalence of new poetic theories—imagism in particular—significantly affected the prose styles of these three novelists. Their allegiance to modern poets and poetry provided the impetus for and the theoretical underpinnings of their prose experiments. Discussion focuses on Hemingway, but notes Faulkner's imagist-inspired poems and outlines the imagist formulations underlying his prose experiments. Quotes *AGB* XXII (#52).

Wasson, Ben. *Count No 'Count: Flashbacks to Faulkner*. Jackson: University Press of Mississippi, 1983.

This memoir by Faulkner's friend of 40 years and sometime agent and editor conveys the intensity and self-awareness with which Faulkner approached his art, especially during his late teens and early twenties. Provides vivid firsthand accounts of the autobiographical impetus for some of Faulkner's poems; of the rivalry between the young, unpublished Faulkner and William Alexander Percy; and of Faulkner's reading aloud the whole of Conrad Aiken's *Turns and Movies* and, later, a Sherwood Anderson story.

_____. "A Memory of Marionettes." In *Marionettes: A Play in One Act*. Oxford, Mississippi: Yoknapatawpha Press, 1975.

Briefly reminisces about poet Faulkner's "Ole Miss" years and provides a history of the 6 (?) hand-bound copies of *TM*.

Wilde, Meta Carpenter and Orin Borsten. *A Loving Gentleman: The Love Story of William Faulkner and Meta Carpenter*. New York: Simon & Schuster, 1976.

Illuminates the very personal role Faulkner's poetry and poet's mask played for him in his relationship with Meta Wilde. Poems quoted are ["Red thy famble"] (#93), ["Se tiarait coup de fusee aimez vous la Francaise"] (#96), and ["I have seen music, heard"] (#51—but see also #159, ["You have seen music, heard"]). See also Brooks 1977, Broughton, Minter, Sensibar 1984, and *Origins*.

Yonce, Margaret. "Faulkner's 'Atthis' and 'Attis': Some Sources of Myth." *MissQ* 23 (Summer 1970): 288–98.

Notes Faulkner's use of *AGB* XVII (#78) in *Soldiers' Pay* and suggests possible sources for his knowledge of the mythical Atthis. Also discussed is *AGB* XXV (#30). See also Brooks 1978 and *Origins*.

_____. "A New Study of Faulkner's First Novel." *MissQ* 36 (Summer 1983): 506–18.

This essay review of Bosha notes the study's neglect of "some of the most important poems which are clearly related to the novel." Briefly discusses poems which Januarius Jones quotes, "On Seeing the Winged Victory for the First Time" (#78) and "Adolescence" (#2), and poems with imagistic links, "L'Apres-Midi d'un Faun" (#7) and *TMF*.

_____. "'Shot Down Last Spring': The Wounded Aviators of Faulkner's Wasteland." *MissQ* 31 (Summer 1978): 359–68.

Gives provenance of "The Lilacs" (#63), notes the influences of early Eliot, and analyzes the poem's themes in relation to "Naiads' Song" (#73) and to *Soldiers' Pay* and *Flags in the Dust*.

Index of Titles and First Lines

Numbers refer to catalogue or figure numbers, not page numbers

DATE DUE

GAYLORD   PRINTED IN U.S.A.